Weaving Our Stories is a drenching of Spirit that helped me remember the shared purpose I have with the world and now with beloved Kalihi, Waipahu, Koʻolauloa, and all of Hawaiʻi. It is indeed an anthology that "...celebrates the radical and revolutionary role stories [play] in supporting our healing and liberation." Mahalo, dear poets, artists, writers, and evolutionary revolutionists, for putting this collection together. Mahalo nui Luanna Peterson for holding the center with the grace of our kupuna – all of them. Time for us to heal. It is an honor to be connected to this kaupapa.

– **Dr. Manu Aluli Meyer**, Indigenous Epistemologist,
   worldwide keynote speaker, and writer

Full of strength and loving provocation, *Weaving our Stories* gathers poems, visual art, and stories of a new generation of Hawaiʻi changemakers. The collection reminds us that we can seek liberation in our ancestral stories; that we reach for liberation by carrying the stories of others; and that we find liberation when we learn and extend the complementary patterns among us. A brilliant representation of Hawaiʻi's own.

– **Dr. Noelani Goodyear-Kaʻōpua,** Professor of Native Hawaiian and
   Indigenous Politics at the University of Hawaiʻi at Mānoa

We are lovingly tethered to each other's struggles, liberation and survival. This is the mantra sweetly embedded across this profound heartfelt body of work. *Weaving our Stories* is a beautifully curated montage of community voices committed to the preservation of their indigenous lands and culture. Here is an anthology that collectively teaches us how to resist, build and dream toward a liberated future. What Luanna Peterson and the contributors offer us is a divine vision to walk with our communities ancestors and descendants with a collective vision to world making. Throughout the anthology lives a chorus of powerful voices that are amplified in a series of interwoven manifestos, stunning visual art and spirited poetics often echoed in their mother tongue. Like strands of sweetgrass, these stories are interlocked and bound up across a multitude of lineages. Hawaiʻi, like many of our homelands, has been a site of settler colonialism, US imperialism and pillaging of its most abundant lands. Every page of *Weaving our Stories* gives us an opportunity to reimagine, regenerate and reclaim our legacies! What *Weaving our Stories* does is make visible the histories and possibilities of freedom for its people and living cultural archive. Upon reading this anthology, I began to realize that each of the contributors in the book serves as a griot of the oral history and creative traditions...which has always been an instrument of change and freedom! Add this to your 2024 booklist.

–**Tarisse Iriarte Medina**, independent curator and consultant
  working in New York City and Puerto Rico

The young leaders and storytellers featured in *Weaving Our Stories* inspire and encourage us to move beyond received narratives that nourish bigotry or diminish one's capacity for compassion and imagination. With powerful pedagogical and artistic impacts, the stories create space for us to name ourselves and heal out loud. The voices simultaneously remember and innovate, as we re-familiarize ourselves with one another as well as 'aina, to weave a tapestry of shared feeling and responsibility. Although the anthology speaks of loneliness and attempted erasure, its words also speak of deep belonging and strength—of the artistry, energy, ingenuity, and wisdom of people, place, and culture; of our commitments to one another; and the healing that comes from washing our eyes – and seeing our truth.

– **Dr. Maya Soetoro-Ng**, Consultant on the International Team
  at the Obama Foundation and a Faculty Specialist
  at the University of Hawai'i

Weaving Our Stories

A Return to Belonging

Edited and with an Introduction by
Luanna Peterson

Daraja Press

Published by Daraja Press
https://darajapress.com
Wakefield, Quebec, Canada

For more information on Weaving Our Stories, contact: ulimovement@gmail.com

ISBN 9781990263903

Cover design: Alisha Kahealani Mahone-Brooks

Library and Archives Canada Cataloguing in Publication

Title: Weaving our stories : a return to belonging / edited and with an introduction by Luanna
    Peterson.
Names: Peterson, Luanna, editor.
Description: Includes bibliographical references.
Identifiers: Canadiana 20230548342 | ISBN 9781990263903 (softcover)
Subjects: LCSH: Literature—Minority authors. | LCSH: Resistance (Philosophy) in literature. |
    LCSH: Art, Modern—21st century.
Classification: LCC PN491.5 .W43 2023 | DDC 808.8/98—dc23

DEDICATION

Weaving our Stories Youth Series Resident Ancestral Guide and Elder

We dedicate this book to Nana Sula. Nana Sula, you were the guiding light, the compass that steered us, and our anchor during our journey together in the youth series. The years 2020-2021 were marked by turbulence, and each day brought new nightmares and fresh challenges to navigate. We witnessed the loss of friends and family, homes, jobs, and sometimes, our sense of stability and hope. The world seemed determined to rock our spirits to the core. Yet, your unwavering love provided a serene haven, enabling each of us to engage in the vital work of Remembering and Returning.

With love, Pūlama, Luanna, and the Weaving Our Stories Youth Series crew.

PREFACE

Dr. Akiemi Glenn, Honolulu-based scholar and culture worker

The collection of writing bound in the *Weaving Our Stories — A Return to Belonging* anthology is doing serious work.

Previous book-length engagements that endeavor to disrupt extractive narratives of Hawai'i have spotlighted academics and the necessary critiques they mount of settler colonialism, Americanism, and imperial militourism. This collection is a welcome continuation of those Hawai'i conversations but also insists on platforming the voices of intersecting contemporary social justice movements and organic intellectuals who challenge ideas of belonging, home, kuleana, memory, and imagination. Editor Luanna Peterson bookends the offerings of nearly 30 contributors with her own grounding introduction and a closing manifesto that sings as a salvo for the complicated work of weaving and untangling that lies ahead for movements for justice.

The chapter headings are signposts for where this work will take us: rooted in cultural memory (Chapter 1), we are called to practice accountability (Chapter 2) in our relationships with ourselves and others so that we can effectively defang the stories imposed on our communities (Chapter 3: Countering Hegemony) and disassemble the social and rhetorical structures that simplify complex worlds and experiences (Chapter 4: Resisting False Binaries). The final chapter features the weaving work of youth participants who have designed creative, joyful, healing, and challenging projects to do with and in communities as they propose experiments and practices that seed the conditions for liberation. The fruits of their imagination work are also the result of relationships with each other, mentors, and various communities in Hawai'i and abroad.

The title and the practice of weaving our stories is the best of metaphor, the word itself from Greek 'meta' (beyond) and 'phero' (to carry). As readers, we observe the voices in this anthology carrying us beyond expectation and sometimes beyond comfort to a place where solidarity is active and reciprocal.

Weaving Our Stories challenges notions of who is in Hawai'i, what they are up to, what they are thinking about, and – most crucially

– how Hawai'i is connected to global movements for Indigenous sovereignty and liberation of oppressed peoples. This collection is notable in that it gives voice to contemporary members of various diasporas not often associated with Hawai'i's post-plantation history and the confluence of a "Local" culture from Indigenous Polynesian, East Asian, and European sources. We hear from Hawai'i-based writers with roots in ka pae 'āina 'o Hawai'i, Sāmoa, Nigeria, Ghana, Algeria, Louisiana, Michigan, Korea, the Philippines, China, California, Mexico, and the Caribbean, plying the strands of their lives and stories of migration, rootedness, and Indigenity with the realities of Native dispossession in occupied Hawai'i. Writers in this anthology step toward the contradictions of their lives and location.

The collection has been curated with a feeling of velocity: short pieces of poetry contrast with memoir-style reflections on identity and community, which contrast again with a lesson plan, a new framework for therapeutic connection, a reverie on intergenerational relationships with plants. Sometimes, the different sizes and shapes of the contributions included can be jarring as disparate positionalities and voices arrive at cross angles to each other in a mounting tension. But, as an editor, Luanna Peterson has shaped this energy in pursuit of her larger aim. Tension is, after all, what makes weaving work. The tension here is active and intentional, the writers of *Weaving Our Stories* demonstrate. It is braced by the relations and structures that have drawn them into community with each other and into this collection of poems, musings, essays, and projects. It supports the continual, careful work of study, reflection, and sharing that this volume exemplifies as an artifact in and of itself. As a practice, we can recognize it as the work of story weaving. Working the metaphor, the weaving here is a steady, deliberate action that deftly manages the ways vulnerable, pliable parts of individual experiences bend in relation to each other. Creating a structure from those flexibilities, story weaving ultimately yields a fabric whose integrity is stronger and more dynamic than the individual strands that made it.

Luanna Peterson's editorial voice intercedes throughout the anthology as a narrator and context builder, weaving with co-collaborator Pūlama Long and their real-life community of youth story weavers and mentors. Peterson closes this collection with an urgency that also pulses throughout the writing in *Weaving Our Stories*. Writing in later 2023, she names how the many global crises of physical violence interweave with narrative violence, speaking directly of the genocides in Palestine, Sudan, and Congo that have been fomented by the storymaking practices of colonizers. Her closing lines are of forgiveness, not of colonizers – never – but between we peoples reckoning with each other, hurting, struggling, learning, committing to imagining a world where we are all truly free. Just like weaving, forgiveness is an intentional action.

Weaving Our Stories – A Return to Belonging is an important literary collection for people committed to social justice in Hawai'i and in the world, not only for the value of individual contributions but because it models a practice of intentionality in building understanding and coordinating action across distance, difference, and time.

–Akiemi Glenn

Raised in the rural US South with genealogical ties to the forests and coastal areas of lands now known North Carolina and Virginia, Dr. Akiemi Glenn is a Honolulu-based scholar and culture worker. As a linguist who works in Indigenous language revitalization, filmmaker, artist, and cultural practitioner, Akiemi's work engages concepts of culture, race, and belonging at the intersections of art, social justice, and education. She is the founder and executive director of the Pōpolo Project, a community organization whose mission is to redefine what it means to be Black in Hawai'i through cultivating connections between individuals, our communities, our ancestors, and the land, highlighting the vivid, complex diversity of Black cultures and identities in the Pacific and around the world.

PROLOGUE

Luanna Peterson, Co-Founder of Weaving Our Stories

fit in here, in my palm, in my shadow, don't be bigger than my idea of you, don't be more beautiful than i can accept, don't be more human than i am willing to allow you to be and be quiet, you're too loud, even your un-belonging is loud. quiet your dreams, your voice, your hair, quiet your skin, quiet your displacement, quiet your longing, your colour, quiet your walk, your eyes. who said you could look at me like that? who said you could exist without permission? why are you even here? why aren't you shrinking? i think of you often. you vibrate. you walk into a room and the temperature changes. i lean in and almost recognize you as human. but, no. we can't have that.

— Warsan Shire

We are born from a multiverse of unique experiences, identities, needs, and desires, and we can co-exist alongside one another, even as our lives, ways of being, and identities diverge. The delineation of our differences and the natural boundaries inherent to the uniqueness of our individual and collective lives need not engender assimilation, othering, and/or marginalization. We can embrace the multitude of diverse stories available to us without falling into an abyss of sameness or othering. I know you can do this because, like me, you were a child once, and you remember for a (brief time) that everyone and every-thing in the world was a friend, no matter how alike or different they were from you.

During my childhood, I shared a deep and unseeable connection with a presence I felt with utmost familiarity. When I use the term "divine," I am not referring to a distant deity perched on a heavenly throne, wielding threats of punishment for disobedience. Instead, I speak of the divine companion known to children, a magical confi-dant. This enchanting companion conversed with me on friendly terms, eternally present in the hues of sunsets, the playfulness of puppies, the fragrance of blooms, and ever alive in the stories that populated my imagination. This divine companion was a master storyteller, narrating tales that left me in awe. My companion unfailingly affirmed my worth and the worth of others. It assured me that I hailed from a lineage of mighty individuals and that I possessed the potential to accomplish extraordinary feats that would reshape the world. This divine friend conveyed that my predecessors, my kin, and my community were luminous heroes, heroines, and shape-shifters, constantly embracing change and growth amidst life's challenges and miracles. The divine companion was, of course, my own inner voice.

Regrettably, as time progressed, that inner voice and my cherished stories began to slip away one after another, yielding space for false narratives to take root. The world presented formidable obstacles to the survival of these age-old tales. I witnessed how those who clung to their authentic stories encountered severe repercussions, including physical harm and banishment. This played out before my eyes in school, as brave kids dared to be true to themselves. I observed it in the challenges my Mother faced when she asserted herself or confronted anti-Black sentiments within our family. I bore witness to the brutal suppression of our narratives so frequently that I chose to mute my stories and my entire voice. These narratives diverged from the enchanting stories of my early years. My aspirations were restricted by the narrators' viewpoints, dictating how far and how high I could aim. These narrators, who had never experienced my life's journey, insisted that my fate was sealed with a life marred by criminality, menial labor, and an appearance deemed inferior, and instincts labeled as savage. You may ask, who were these narrators? They emerged from the ranks of politicians, media outlets, employers, textbooks, the medical field, educators, banking institutions, law enforcement, urban planners, unfamiliar faces, family members, friends, passing strangers – a vast array of individuals, communities, and institutions swayed by a privileged few to believe that our existence held no significance outside of pleasing the whims of the rich and powerful.

❀

As the years went by, I was expected to beg or steal a seat at the table of life or watch with envy as the *belonged (the rooted and welcomed)* enjoyed the fruits of life freely and with ease. The stories that replaced my most cherished stories were now one-dimensional, fatalistic, and built on a foundation of lies. In these new stories, my family and I were the *'unbelonged'*. We were the strange, the unfathomable, the abnormal due to our skin color, economic caste, generational displacement, zip code, and any other category that fell outside the white hetero, well-to-do male station. Falling prey to these narratives, I began to act in ways that unwittingly validated their claims, like a self-fulfilling prophecy too potent to evade. I grew defiant, desperate, solitary, consumed by rage and bent on destruction. I sought escape by running away, I defied authority as a matter of principle, and I cared little for the place and people that were, in truth, my home.

Fortunately, seeds of belonging took root again in high school when my youth parole officer mandated that I attend the Leeward YMCA every day after school in Waipahu, a neighborhood beset with an abundance of racist and classist false narratives for as long as I can remember. The Leeward Y, under the guidance of dedicated Program Leaders including Grandma Nette—who would later become my hānai mother—Uncle Loso, Aunty Gloria, and Aunty Lori, offered programs that nurtured a genuine love for our community. These mentors emphasized the celebration of our diverse cultures and histories, while creating opportunities for us to express our voices and agency.

Although some excursions might have been beyond our financial reach, our community spirit and agency proved invaluable. On Grandma Nette's driveway, we ingeniously placed an empty garbage can, inviting our neighbors to contribute whatever spare change they could offer. In exchange, they became part of a Polynesian voyage that unfolded on that cool black tar driveway, under the embrace of the twinkling night sky as our hips swayed to the rhythm of the ocean and archived the ancient stories our bodies conveyed. The money collected allowed us to journey to the outer islands and on rare occasions to the continent, deepening our understanding of the world we inhabited. Most importantly, we witnessed the tangible outcomes of our collective agency – a realization that our actions could shape our reality in meaningful ways.

✿

On our school lunch breaks, we confronted challenges directly beneath the comforting shade of the mango tree, all the while guided by the wisdom of Uncle Loso. His stories of childhood in Samoa, intricately woven with profound insights, breathed life into our own journey of growing up in an American-occupied Hawai'i. Within a landscape where perceptions of normalcy were perpetually intertwined with whiteness, we collectively arrived at the understanding that our struggles weren't inherently tied to our identities.

And, there was Aunty Lori. Aunty took us on journeys around the island in the large white YMCA van, narrating haunting stories of places we frequented but barely knew. In the back of the van, gripping the edges of our seats, we learned of Pele's transformation into an elderly woman with flowing white hair. She tested the empathy of those who passed her, appearing as a hitchhiker along the roadside. Dismissing Pele's needs or failing to treat her with aloha could summon unimaginable catastrophe.

Meanwhile, Aunty Gloria, with her nurturing guidance, held us accountable to ourselves and each other with her warm yet assertive demeanor. Aunty Gloria's "stink eye" steered us back to our moral center whenever we veered off course. As we stumbled through the awkward process of mastering the *ami* or slap dance, Aunty Gloria shot us a stink eye as she watched us shame our own and each other's perceived shortcomings. Aunty Gloria would recount stories of heroes who chose the path of moral integrity, even when it meant forsaking personal comfort. She reminded us that our hips swayed to the rhythm of the ocean and was an archive of the ancient stories our bodies conveyed and that this was no laughing matter. Recognizing that our self-deprecation during this learning journey could harm something much bigger than our pride, we embraced our vulnerability, fostering a collective strength that bound us together in unity and resilience.

Where once we were ashamed of our Waipahu, we now represented our community with fierce pride. We were not one-dimensional at-risk kids from the "hood." We had our own stories, which could only form through our Belonging, through someone bearing witness to our lives. In our shared belonging, we owned, exchanged, and celebrated our stories and cultural memories. In this, we found opportunities to evolve and celebrate our individual and collective well-being.

Though the youth and our adult mentors would continue to grapple with internalized racism, colorism, sexism, and the myriad "isms" inherent in living under the sway of whiteness, at least, for a fleeting moment, we could find solace in our own skin. The mango tree's embrace offered us a space where our diverse identities harmoniously coexisted, reminding us that unity in our shared human experience transcended the oppressive narratives that sought to divide us.

Since then, I've actively sought out opportunities to share the invaluable lessons I acquired during my formative years at the YMCA. I actively search for stories that amplify our voices and challenge the misleading narratives that rob us of our inherent worth and displace us from our rightful place in the world. The *Weaving Our Stories: Return To Belonging* Anthology celebrates the radical and revolutionary role stories in supporting our healing and liberation. Many thanks to our youth series participants and community supporters for the generous gift of your story.

At the conclusion of this book, you will find "An Unyielding Truth: A Manifesto for Global Liberation." The decision to place this manifesto here is both intentional and necessary, given the rapidly evolving global landscape since the writing of this book.

In the time that has passed, the world has witnessed an intensification of atrocities and injustices across various regions. The escalation of conflicts and the deepening of humanitarian crises have brought forth a stark reality – the issues discussed within these pages are not just historical accounts or theoretical discussions; they are urgent, living realities that continue to unfold in real-time.

This manifesto is a call to action in a world increasingly defined by strife and exploitation. This final argument underscores the urgency and relevance of the themes explored throughout the book. It is a reminder that the fight for justice, equality, and the recognition of the intrinsic worth of all life and land is an ongoing struggle that demands our immediate attention and action.

As you reach the end of this journey through the book, "An Unyielding Truth: A Manifesto For Global Liberation" is presented not as a conclusion but as a beginning – an invitation to join a global movement towards liberation and justice. It is a clarion call that resonates beyond the final pages, urging each of us to carry its message into our lives and communities, transforming thought into action.

INTRODUCTION

Weaving Our Stories, a Return to Belonging

Our histories never unfold in isolation. We cannot truly tell what we consider to be our own histories without knowing the other stories. And often we discover that those other stories are actually our own stories.

– Angela Y. Davis

Weaving Our Stories originated from a shared aspiration for the emancipation of all oppressed communities in Hawai'i and beyond. Our inspiration drew from our involvement in the Huliāmahi Alliance, a Native Hawaiian educational land-based initiative in He'eia, Hawai'i. Co-founder Pūlama Long and I observed our narratives' transformative impact on our communities collective well-being. Paying close attention to the stories of the land, the stories of our students, teachers, families, and cultural practitioners, and the various points where their stories converged and diverged allowed for a more nuanced approach to the design and delivery of our educational programming. Moreover, we saw that these stories had the power to amplify social justice work as they revealed hidden histories, reframed power dynamics, and offered space for a true account of our lived experiences.

The Huliāmahi Alliance alliance comprises three Native Hawaiian-led non-profit organizations dedicated to land stewardship, situated in the He'eia ahupua'a on O'ahu: Papahana Kuaola, Kāko'o 'Ōiwi, and Paepae o He'eia. These organizations strategically span the entire He'eia ahupua'a, from the uplands represented by Papahana Kuaola to the coastal expanse overseen by Paepae o He'eia. The ahupua'a, a land management system, typically extends from mountain peaks to coastal areas, serving as a cohesive unit that varies based on topography, elevation, moisture, and available resources. What unifies the ahupua'a concept across diverse landscapes is a shared social framework rooted in values that foster the interconnectedness and prosperity of both the land and its people (Beamer, 79).

Our educational approach at the alliance was rooted in the guiding principle known as Aloha ʻĀina. This concept teaches us that when we cultivate aloha, or love, for the land and hold a mindful awareness of its finite resources, we engage in a reciprocal relationship. By speaking the Mother tongue of the indigenous peoples who have nurtured an enduring connection with the land for generations, we foster a symbiosis that allows us not only to endure but to flourish. In this context, the notion of unbelonging is nonexistent. The concept of ʻotherʼ dissolves. Everyone, every story, every lesson, every animate and inanimate entity within the ahupuaʻa finds its place and purpose. Belonging, in its essence, has always been intrinsic to our survival.

Students were offered the opportunity to nurture this profound relationship with both the land and its people. This was achieved through active involvement in the sites, under the expert guidance of cultural practitioners at each location. Additionally, stories or moʻolelo intricately connected each of the three sites to a comprehensive framework, elevating values and ways of being that safeguarded the well-being of the land and the people whose lives depended on it.

We were driven by the profound relationship and responsibility we hold towards the sovereign nation of Hawaiʻi, seeking to unveil learning models and best practices that nurture the land's well-being and the holistic wellness of individuals and the communities intertwined with the land. Our sacred bond with the land mirrors a familial contract, as we are entrusted with loving, safeguarding, nurturing, and imparting wisdom to the ensuing generations. The wisdom of our elders, who sustain us with their devotion to our welfare, fuels our understanding. Similarly, the land, our venerable ancestral link, carries the cultural heritage that our forebears carry and pass down to guide future generations. Much like our elders' living memories, the land narrates a living saga that reminds us of our interconnectedness and shared responsibility as a family.

The students we worked with at Huliāmahi would often go home to their families and share stories of ancient Hawaiian fishponds and sacred springs in Waipao. They saw for themselves what it meant for their well-being and the well-being of their community when they spent a day helping to restore an ancient fishpond so that it could continue to provide food for their community. Once, at the fishpond,

Pūlama told her students about their ancestral kin who lived on the land they called home: brilliant warriors, fishermen, navigators, teachers, priests, and more. For many, it was the first time they heard stories that reflected the countless accomplishments of their people. Students experienced a sense of pride they had never experienced in their continent-issued textbooks. They learned skills passed down through the generations with academic, cultural, social-emotional, and spiritual value. Moreover, the exchange of stories between the classroom teachers and our cultural practitioners revealed shared values, clarified assumptions, and allowed for creative solutions to barriers encountered in the delivery of Aloha ʻĀina education in Western-dominated educational systems through an exchange of innovative pedagogical models.

Western white-male hegemonic power deprioritizes narratives that challenge political, economic, and cultural domination, effectively silencing the voices of oppressed peoples. Those benefiting from and upholding this hegemony center on a singular narrative that elevates their power, aspirations, and worldview, often disregarding other stories, truths, and lives. We reject the perpetuation of this narrative. To collectively confront humanity's myriad challenges, we must embrace narratives encompassing diverse truths. In our pursuit of survival, we must engage with stories reflecting varied ways of existence and knowledge, including the stories of the land and the rich cultures of all peoples.

Consider the impact when a young child from historically marginalized communities, traditionally stripped of their influence and agency, returns home to share that their people have historically been scientists, engineers, and expert navigators. Visualize the far-reaching ripples that spread as these stories are conveyed. Imagine the transformative effect when these young minds desire to uncover their ancestral origins, asking to hear their grandparents' tales of stewarding the land. Envision this child discovering a sense of belonging within these narratives. What follows in your imagination as this journey continues?

In the essay *Teaching Amid U.S. Occupation: Sovereignty, Survival, and Social Studies in a Native Hawaiian Charter School featured* in the journal Hülili: Multidisciplinary Research on Hawaiian Well-Being, Hawaiian educators and scholars underscore the cultural, economic, and political impact of Aloha ʻĀina education:

> We believe that all education is political, whether or not the teachers and students are conscious of the politics embedded in the learning. To be Hawaiian in Hawaiʻi, to maintain our distinct culture and collective identity as a people, is political. To speak our language, once banished by those who established the illegal U.S. occupation, is a political gesture. By reliving our cultural protocols and giving breath to our oli, we have already engaged in the political struggle to enrich our lāhui Hawaiʻi and restore national pride. As Kumu, aloha ʻāina starts with us. And yet the hegemonic cultural, economic, and political systems occupying our islands operate in ways that are antithetical to the ethics and practices of aloha ʻāina and mālama ʻāina. Consequently, becoming an educator advocating for Hawaiian cultural values and traditions is undoubtedly political. (*Goodyear-Kaʻōpua, Noelani, et al. 178*)

Stories can amplify voices that have been critical to the possibility of change but are pushed to the margin in favor of top-down hegemonic narratives. During my time at Huliāmahi, we harvested stories from our participants and stakeholders– staff, teachers, and parents that spoke of challenges and barriers as well as of renewal and transformation. We saw that the moʻolelo of the ʻāina and the everyday stories of our teachers, students, cultural practitioners, and the ʻāina served a critical function in the success of our program and, thus, the wellbeing of our community. In the Hawaiian worldview, moʻolelo serves a function beyond entertainment. Moʻolelo is not just a story for the sake of being a story. Unlike your traditional Disney story, whose primary goal is to entertain, the function of moʻolelo, much like the function of stories in many Black, Brown, and Indigenous communities throughout the world, is to transmit and activate beliefs, customs, practices, genealogy, and ways of being that support our relationship and responsibility to place, self, family, and community. Unfortunately, pervasive and oppressive narratives have usurped our own moʻolelo for generations.

From Seed to Bloom

I aspired to harness the transformative power of our narratives and channel it into social and political forms of resistance, uniting diverse communities of color across Hawai'i and beyond. Hawai'i stands as one of the world's most culturally diverse locales, primarily due to settler occupation following an unlawful overthrow of the sovereign Hawaiian kingdom that introduced missionaries, white businessmen, forced labor economies in plantations, military installations, tourism, and a continuous influx of displaced individuals from various corners of the globe, driven by American hegemonic influences. While not everyone's story in Hawai'i, this is the reality for many.

Despite the rich tapestry of people coexisting here, numerous communities remain separated by impenetrable divides. I believe in the value of fellowship—each individual, culture, community, and identity carries its uniqueness, drawing individuals together based on shared experiences and ways of life. Boundaries can establish secure havens for fellowship, nurturing a sense of belonging and well-being. Yet, these boundaries need not breed a sense of 'otherness' or false superiority. It's entirely possible to cultivate understanding and invest in one another's welfare across identity lines, especially when acknowledging that many of us confront the label of 'other' within the framework of white supremacy. As of 2019, Hawai'i's white population stood at 25%, compared to the United States' 76% white population. Hawai'i is characterized as a "majority-minority" state. The term "minority" comprises various racial categories—Black, American Indian, Asian, Pacific Islander, Other, and two or more races (esri. com)—but excludes "white alone." At the very least, we all share a common narrative of being marginalized, excluded, and dehumanized due to our perceived 'otherness.' While our specific experiences may differ, there's a point where our stories converge across time and space. It's also undeniable that our shared humanity holds significance.

As the world braced itself against the tumultuous currents of change during the start of the global COVID pandemic, the stories that wove themselves into our collective tapestry between 2020 and 2021 took on new dimensions. Just as threads of protest movements ignited from Hawai'i to Hong Kong, weaving a fabric of global dissent against systemic injustices, our local landscape bore witness to impassioned voices and powerful standoffs. While kia'i gathered to protect the sacred Mauna Kea and challenge the encroachment of development, a larger struggle for truth and justice unfolded on a global stage. Simultaneously, as the resonance of truth seemed to be silenced by the cacophony of misinformation, the urgency for unity, healing, and transformation became ever more palpable.

We saw protest movements igniting all over the world. From Hawai'i to India, Iraq to Los Angeles, Venezuela to Zimbabwe, Haiti to Puerto Rico, and Hong Kong to Colombia, people were taking to the streets to express their grievances against systemic and structural injustices. At home that summer, kia'i gathered to block a road at the base of Mauna Kea, and more than 30 elders were arrested.[1] Trump was trumping the truth anytime he had a mic or social media platform to spout from. If Trump was a singular man, he might have been manageable. Unfortunately, the Trumps of the world were flinging their destructive power and ideology in every direction, as they had been for hundreds of years, and their efforts seemed to be wildly intensifying. The world had had enough. Their time was up.

On March 13, 2020, police murdered 26-year-old Breonna Taylor as she slept peacefully in bed. Not long after, the world watched footage on May 25, 2020, of George Floyd, under the knee of a white officer, crying, "I can't breathe" in Minneapolis, Minnesota. According to a report done by the Washington Post, police shot and killed at least 1,055 people nationwide in 2021 and 1,021 people in 2020 (Bunn). According to Mapping Police Violence, Black people, who account for 13 percent of the U.S. population, represented 27 percent of those killed by police in 2021.

In August of 2021, Julian Heyward III was found hanged on his lānai at his home in Ha'ikū, Maui. His death followed a history of conflict with his landlord and disputes about rent after Julian experienced economic hardship at the height of the COVID-19 pandemic.

1 As of the date of this writing, the 29 kūpuna who were arrested on Mauna Kea in 2019 had their cases dismissed by the federal court. (https://www.staradvertiser.com/2022/04/02/hawaii-news/cases-dismissed-for-mauna-kea-kupuna/)

During this time, Julian experienced anti-Black racism, including threats of physical harm that he reported to his family and the authorities. Despite the police reports and the proceedings he filed against his landlord, who sought to evict him during a statewide eviction moratorium, Maui police quickly ruled his death by hanging a suicide.

On April 5, 2021, Honolulu police officer Geoffrey Thom fired ten rounds at Micronesian 16-year-old Iremamber Sykap. A few weeks later, on April 14, officers with Honolulu Police Department shot and killed unarmed South African Oʻahu resident Lindani Myeni. Myeni had been leaving a home he mistook for a Hari Krishna temple when several police officers confronted him in the dark without identifying themselves. Myeni attempted to defend himself against unknown assailants (he asked twice who they were) and was tased and shot four times. In both instances, the murders were found to be justifiable, with the Honolulu Police Department claiming they had no choice but to kill.

During that period, a surge of support, curiosity, and sometimes disdain for Black liberation movements emerged in Hawaiʻi. Communities rallied together to back Black liberation endeavors with acts of solidarity that stood as poignant examples. Notably, young Black students and their allies orchestrated protests that drew around 10,000 supporters, commemorating the lives lost due to racial injustice on the continent (Lee). However, paradoxically, alongside these demonstrations of unity and resistance, a denial emerged regarding the presence of similar issues within Hawaiʻi. Two opposing camps surfaced: one dismissing anti-Blackness in a supposed post-racial Hawaiʻi, deeming Black social justice movements irrelevant; the other discrediting Black lives, asserting that such movements and the Black community held no place in Hawaiʻi. This dichotomy revealed how entrenched false narratives could be, leading individuals to align more comfortably with their oppressors than with the truth. Caravans bearing the Aloha ʻĀina flag and the blue lives matter flag, symbolizing police's role in maintaining order, traversed neighborhoods. Despite their shared display, the blue lives matter movement, with ties to white nationalists and hate groups, emerged as a counter to Black liberation movements (Chammah And Aspinwall). Interestingly, these groups displayed minimal concern for Hawai'i's illegal occupation, desecration of sacred sites, or the worldwide marginalization of people of color.

In Hawai'i, overt anti-Black sentiment surged across streets, workplaces, and social media platforms. Paradoxically, despite visible incidents, the narrative persisted that Hawai'i was a racial utopia. Strikingly, the rhetoric used to discredit Black social justice movements echoed the rhetoric used against movements advocating justice, sovereignty, and self-determination for Kanaka Maoli and other BIPOC communities. This convergence of language illustrated how we were inadvertently employing the language of our oppressors and weaving false narratives against those victimized by the same oppression we aimed to end.

Certain colleagues and educators hesitated to engage in conversations about anti-Blackness or America's illegal occupation of Hawai'i. Exploring these issues in the context of white supremacy and their impact on Hawai'i's educational system could have been transformative. Examining the roots of injustices in Hawai'i might have illuminated how white supremacy and its enforcement mechanisms—racism, manifest destiny, colonialism, imperialism, occupation, capitalism, eurocentric education, and environmental degradation—rely on creating an inferior opposite on the spectrum: Blackness. Anyone non-white is seen as approaching or embodying Blackness, resulting in perceptions of difference, inferiority, and vulnerability to subjugation. Therefore, white supremacy, colonization, and Western hegemonic occupation hinge on anti-Blackness. Educators, by considering students' experiences as both victims and witnesses of anti-Black racism, could have explored the educational, social, and emotional ramifications of such encounters.

Discussing the relevance and existence of Blackness in Hawai'i and the Pacific, both historically and in contemporary contexts, along with acknowledging our roles as victims and witnesses of anti-Black racism, has proven to be challenging. Fear of the unknown often impedes meaningful relationships with those perceived as 'other' or unfamiliar. This fear obstructs meaningful connections with the 'other,' resulting in misrepresentations. Whether driven by fear or a false sense of superiority, individuals fill gaps in understanding with stereotypical tropes and oppressive language, crafting inaccurate narratives about themselves and others. These manufactured stories position 'othered' communities as simultaneously invisible—devoid of significance, belonging, or contributions—and hyper-visible—subject to unwarranted scrutiny, portraying them as threats or scapegoats. This dual rendering of 'othered' peoples as invisible and hyper-visible is initiated by dominant power structures (white capitalist institutions/ communities/individuals), and this behavior is often replicated within marginalized communities to maintain whatever level of power their respective identities afford.

Growing up in Waipahu, I absorbed crucial lessons that still guide me today. I gained insights into my identity, family, neighbors, and peers whose roots span the Pacific and the globe. I learned about diverse ways of existence, and knowing that positively shaped my growth. However, our relationships with our identities and the expe- riences of those from different communities often conflicted with false narratives that reinforced the supposed inferiority of 'othered' peoples. Corner stores peddled skin-whitening products, the media propagated the supremacy of whiteness, and some, not all, trans- planted teachers treated Black and Brown students as presumed culprits. We noticed that melanin-rich individuals typically (though not universally) resided in economically challenged communities like Waipahu.

In contrast, predominantly East-Asian and white communities were found (though not universally) primarily in more affluent areas such as Hawai'i Kai, Kailua, and Kahala. Our material conditions and the stories propagated by the media shaped our perceptions; we experienced law enforcement's treatment, school environments, and other institutions designed to safeguard us. Generations had been subjected to racist textbooks that omitted our stories and contribu- tions. Over time, we internalized the stories that cast ourselves and others as inferior.

Classmates, some of whom, like my own family, had endured generations of virulent white racism, delighted in using racial slurs against me. Micronesian students faced relentless bullying, and

Filipino students were labeled as "fobs" despite their generations-long presence in Hawai'i. Ironically, those we cast as 'other' reflected our shared struggles with racism and marginalization. These 'others' looked much like us, yet we distanced ourselves from them due to their perceived danger, backwardness, or difference. They were inferior due to slightly darker (or so we perceived) skin, kinkier hair, or accents revealing their family's recent or distant arrivals from Fiji, Micronesia, the Philippines, or other melanin-rich regions impacted by US colonization and occupation. Our experiences of invisibility and hyper-visibility varied depending on our perceived proximity to Blackness. False narratives of inferiority, perpetuated by individuals and oppressive systems, fueled conflicts, exclusion, and exploitation in classrooms, social circles, workplaces, streets, and homes.

In June of 2020, in response to the then chief of the Honolulu Police Department, Susan Ballard's statement that there was less racial bias in Hawai'i, Civil Beat journalist Anita Hofschneider shared data that revealed a disturbing but true story of the lived experiences of people of color in Hawai'i. In her report, Hofschneider shares the following data contradicting the racial utopia myth put forward by Susan Ballard and many others:

> "If anything, implicit bias in Hawai'i is just as strong as on the mainland," says Justin Levinson, a professor at the University of Hawai'i William S. Richardson School of Law. In one study, he found participants who were Hawai'i residents had far more anti-Micronesian bias compared with non-Hawai'i residents. Anti-Blackness is present here too.
>
> In a 2010 study, Levinson and his colleague Danielle Young showed participants images of a burglary suspect. In some pictures, the suspect had light skin; in others, he had dark skin. Participants were far more likely to judge a crime suspect as guilty and evidence as indicating guilt if the subject was presented as dark-skinned than if he were light-skinned, even if they were only shown the photo briefly.
>
> "Skin tone alone, without group identification, led to these effects," Levinson and fellow researchers wrote in a later summary of the analysis.

Native Hawaiians and other Pacific Islanders were the subject of 33% of HPD use-of-force incidents in 2018. They make up about 10% of the state population or as much as 26% if you include people who are multiracial.

For the past 10 years, Hawai'i's Black community consistently was the subject of about 7% of HPD use-of-force incidents annually. They make up just 2.2% of the state population, or about 3.8% if you include people who are part-Black.

In contrast, Asian people were far less likely to be on the receiving end of the police force in Honolulu compared with their proportion of the population. (Hofschneider)

A note to the reader—this is just a snapshot of the injustices people of color face in Hawai'i. Please take some time to research the ongoing injustices enacted against Kanaka Maoli due to the ongoing occupation of the sovereign Hawaiian nation and the ongoing injustices against Black, Indigenous, and people of color in Hawai'i due to the ongoing hegemony of White Supremacy here and everywhere.

The Launch of the Weaving Our Stories 2020-2021 Youth Series

In September 2020, Weaving Our Stories embarked on a journey of collaboration with six young Black organizers, embarking on a year-long immersive experience combining virtual workshops, community engagements, and mentorships. The Weaving Our Stories Youth Series acted as a catalyst for societal transformation, interweaving individual narratives with a comprehensive analysis of the larger communities to which we belong. This initiative prompted participants and the wider communities we engaged with to bear witness to stories spanning both within and outside our spheres, challenging prevailing false narratives. This collective endeavor uncovered shared aspirations for change and proactive measures. Our program's foundation rested on ancestral wisdom, the cultural knowledge of participants and facilitators, personal tales of resistance, the pillars of liberation that emerged from our resistance, and the values and insights of our host peoples, the Kanaka Maoli.

Initially, our vision for this anthology was to spotlight the experiences and culminating works of our 2020-2021 Youth Series participants. However, we expanded this vision to encompass our broader BIPOC community, encouraging their inclusion of stories of resistance. These stories align with our four themes of resistance: cultural memory, accountability, challenging false binaries, and countering hegemony.

Weaving Our Stories Youth Series offered an inclusive roadmap to liberation spanning our diverse communities. Our program was meticulously designed to employ the power of storytelling, guided dialogues, and ancestral weaving techniques, all contributing to enriching community bonds on Oʻahu. Our approach simultaneously addressed collective healing, individual empowerment, and transformative growth. Rooted in Hawaiʻi's landscape, our workshops were grounded in kanaka ʻōiwi (Hawaiian) wisdom, magnified through the lens of traditional Hawaiian weaving practices and the profound insights of ulana lauhala (weaving). This physical connection intertwines seamlessly with the intellectual aspects of Hawaiian knowledge, values, and the sacred kuleana (responsibility) we hold towards our land and the diverse narratives of our Black, Brown, and Indigenous communities.

To our readers, we hope these stories kindle your spirit of resistance, rekindle the sense of innate belonging within you, and inspire you to treasure and safeguard your narratives of resistance and liberation.

OUR STORIES OF RESISTANCE

Chapters are organized according to each of our four themes of resistance: Cultural memory, Accountability, Countering Hegemony, and Resisting False binaries. Each chapter will begin with our understanding of each theme in the context of our resistance and liberation.

CHAPTER 1
Cultural Memory

Hala Pahu by David Akeo

Cultural Memory is a magic carpet ride. I worked on this drum for years, but I never used it until now. I remember now. I use kaula cordage for the pahu. The plants in the background are hala.

There is a danger of a single story. No one is a single story. –
Chimamanda Ngozi Adichie

Dear reader, I want to know who you are. Are you the Bad Boy? Are you the Damsel in Distress? Are you La Femme Fatale? Are you the Girl or Boy Next Door? Are you the Hooker with a Heart of Gold? Are you the Thug? Are you a Queen? Are you the Immigrant? Are you Prince Charming? Are you the Straight Man? I imagine you are probably vigorously shaking your head as you scream at the page, "No! Absolutely not! I am more than a trope!" You are correct. There is no way for me to understand you without you. I need you here; I need your voice. I need the story of you to be authored by you. We often depend on these one-dimensional tropes to understand the 'other' and, often, even ourselves. Remembering the truth of who we are and doing the work to unpack and interrogate long-held cultural assumptions is difficult work. But clinging to false narratives limits the reach of our imagination and our potential for change.

We invite you to remember. Remember the stories housed in your molecular memory. Remember the stories hidden in your Grandmother's recipes. Find the stories that set the record straight. Most of the stories we access, whether via mainstream news outlets, on Hollywood screens, in our school textbooks, or on social media, are not our or your stories. These stories are crafted to reproduce power and privilege through performance and consumption. These stories rarely tell the truth and are one-dimensional binary allegories: Us vs. Them. He vs. She. Black vs. White. Rich vs. Poor. Right vs. Wrong. Winner vs. Loser.

Look for the stories of the land, our ancestors, your yesterdays, and today; reach for stories that speak for all of our relations. Reach for stories that go back to the beginning of time. These stories contain a blueprint for our survival and evolution. Our cultural memory holds stories that reveal ways of being that brought generations of peace and abundance. Remember, we existed long before contact, long before the occupation, and long before Capitalism turned your story into a hashtag. Ask yourself: What stories have been concealed for cultural hegemony to survive? Who has benefited from this forgetting?

Remember, too, those stories that reveal ways of being that promise torment and destruction. These stories have also been stricken from our memory or rewritten in ways that benefit those who have gained the most from our suffering. Forgotten are the horrors of Rome, the slave trade, the Crusades, Hitler, Jim Crow, George Otto Gey, diseases that wiped out entire tribes, U.S.-backed coups, broken treaties, occupation of sovereign lands, et al.

So, now here we are. Solutions to our most pressing problems draw from a memory missing the most important lessons that can heal and change lives. We must harvest lessons from our beautiful, brilliant, life-affirming stories. We also need lessons that can be distilled from the dark stories of our past, stories that can help everyone to understand the consequences of our short-sighted actions.

May we remember the complexity, depth, breadth, beauty, truth, and the necessity of our stories. We challenge you to remember. Pick up your pen and let the forgotten road return to you.

The following stories counter the stockpiles of stories that have been forced onto our psyches and communities for far too long. They are here to correct the record; they are a call to remember. We invite you to respond with recollections of your genius, deep sightings (Bambara), ancestral memories, rooted memories, and truth.

Artist statement: *My submission speaks to the cultural memory that is inherent in all of us, whether we grew up connected to our peoples or not. Like ancestral trauma, we also carry ancestral knowledge & healing. Those are the things I hope to remind us of through this piece.*
— Pumehana Cabral

Remembering Our Future

I felt Hawai'i before I was born. She called my blood and bones back home. My ears remembered my great-grandmother's voice when she spoke 'Ōlelo Hawai'i, even though I never heard her. I knew that three generations later I would call Kailua home as she did. My eyes remembered what Kawainui Marsh looked like when it was a loko i'a, a fishpond connecting us from miles inland to the ocean [see photo below].

My hands remember the lo'i that sprawled across our 'āina, mud so nourishing that we could eat it. My feet remember the sand untouched

Fig. 4. KAWAINUI POND AND WET-LAND CULTIVATION SEEN FROM THE "NEW PALI ROAD." Photo by Brother Bertram, ca. 1898. Hawai'i State Archives, Brother Bertram Coll.

*Source: https://www.hookuaaina.org/moolelo-makalei/

by colonizers and plastic and debris of this century. I remember centuries before I existed, when I was a dream in the minds and hearts of my kūpuna. I remember how they prayed for us, and how they took care of our honua. My voice remembers our oli and moʻolelo, even if I haven't learned them yet – just like I remember what our future generations will look like, what they will see, what they will hear, what they will feel.

I remember how our mountains and waters will flourish. I see how all the lands across our pae ʻāina will be restored – alongside our ea, alongside the sovereignty of all Native peoples. I hear the mele of our great-great-grandchildren and their great-great-grandchildren. I feel them lifting me up when I become their kupuna, trusting my guidance, sending me their pule, and speaking to me through the winds.

Artist Statement: *I have only recently discovered how powerful words can be. For a long time, I had no love for words. I saw them as strictly utilitarian, as others would view a sidewalk or grocery store. I would carelessly curse myself daily with poisonous and destructive slurs. The numbing effect was at first welcomed but would later hurt more than the pain it masked. It would be much later until the beautiful souls of kānaka ʻōiwi professors and unselfish Indigenous women taught me that words are truly magic; that vulnerability is a strength; and that telling our stories is a returning of ourselves back into the past and assuring our place in the future. Now I use storytelling as medicine, working through my personal, generational, and ancestral trauma. Pain is a familiar friend I no longer hide but embrace as part of my life. Others taught me this, and now I wish to help those who no longer want to exist in numbness.*

– Gabriel Verduzco

Grandma's Kitchen

Her name is rosemary
and the cocina is the only place
She's known to be home.
To call it a warzone
 or anything other than home,
is an extreme lack of understanding of cooking
and a lack of understanding of rosemary.

It's where anger and pettiness dissipate,
and where love and peace begin,
where arguments over owed money are immediately squashed
for the time being, when there's pozole in the pot.

Her prized possession isn't the dull knives
she's had for thirty years,
or the one big copper pot.

It's the molcajete
from which my great great great great ancestors
made and used.

The same one I wish to inherit.
They say a knife is a chef's best friend
but they've never seen this chingona
use a mortar and pestle and an old gas stove top.
The mere presence of it is enough
to pull the biggest Oakland Raiders fan
away from the game.

They know my abuelas heart will soon be manifested in
the combination of freshly ground spices and herbs,
the watery guts spilling from the char-roasted sweet,
     velvety green tomatillos
and the even more Blackened red crunchy dried pimientos,
leaving just a child-sized handful
of good mouth-numbing seeds in.
This holy ground is where I learned the meaning of patience
     and love.
Instead of an apple,
it came from making Oaxacan Chicken Mole Negro.

Brown Girl

Brown Girl I choose you not just for your pozole soul
Or that your cheeks fill with the warm hue of a Mexican prickly pear.

Not even for the fact that your hair is as old and wise as obsidian.

But you embody bravery, love, devotion, healing, power, sex,
     strength, and beauty. You are the huitzilli or hummingbird
     for you anglos.

There's a reason why you ain't ever seen a hummingbird in the
     hands of man, un-cageable.

Seeing you, I know why the caged bird sings, because most of us
     will never break free but you fly so high in the sky even though
     they poisoned it with white supremacy.

Keep flyin' girl, it's your destiny, get you a piece of that pie and
     don't ever let a mother fucka question you

why
when all they do is justify your reason to die,
You got time today but fuck em anyway.

You were born to bring light in this world, that's true,
you have the audacity to do the impossible,
make things possible, that's hope, damn that shit gangsta

Artist Statement: *I began this art series after a conversation I had with my grandfather, who emigrated from Punjab, India, to the United States. While sharing old family pictures of my great grandparents and grandparents, we discussed the 1984 Sikh Genocide, the chaos and destruction that caused the entire state of Punjab, and the trauma this caused to the Sikh psyche. My nana ji and nani ji (maternal grandfather and grandmother) and many elders of their generation knew time by what came before 1984 and then what happened after 1984. 1984 was cyclical, but so was 1947 when the partition divided what is now called India and Pakistan. This was when my great-grandparents had to leave their homes and seek refuge in an unknown place.*

These events left questions of what came before life and what came after death for me as an artist. My grandparents and many elders of their generation knew the time in this way. Time was conceptualized by an event that left a permanent mark in the body of my elders that reflects the narrative I share in my work. In my work, I am creating abstractions of "piecing together" the body of the women that I belong to. My art practice is based on preserving the stories of the women that came before me through somatic remembrance of ancestral practices through reimagined mythologies. It is all too often that these stories and histories become lost. We must remember that they are essential to our survival.

– Navjeet Kaur

Blood Memories:
Of Sun, Soil, and Threaded Rivers

"Piecing Her Together / An Offering"
Oils on Wooden Panel with Watercolor Collage and Clay Candles
48 x 24 inches
2020

"Connected"
Watercolor, Charcoal, and Black Tea on paper
24 x 18 inches
2020

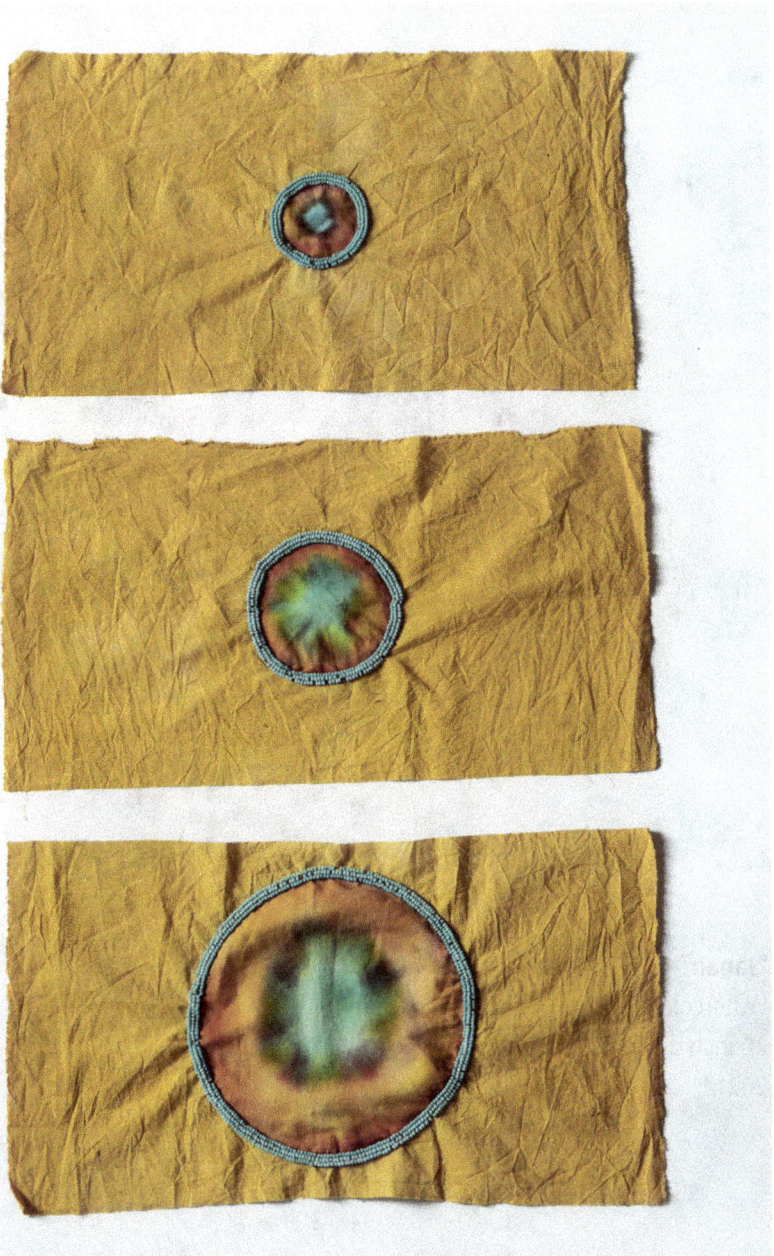

"Womb Bath"
Hand-Dyed with Plant Materials and Embroidered Glass Beads
14 x 25 inches each
2021

"Janan"
Watercolor, Ink, and Plant Dyes on paper
20 inch diameter
2021

Artist Statement: *Pondering on the Black existence, especially when those roots were ripped from us so prematurely, has severed our active relationship with our ancestors and the natural world. This piece was reflective of the Juneteenth celebration on Oʻahu in 2020. Cultural memory is a driving force to combat the violence of white supremacy/ hegemony.*

– Jade Rhodes

We came to the water.
An Ode to Juneteenth

We came to the water,
to heal
but water for Black folx has always been two sides of a coin:
Liberation, subjugation.

We came to the water,
those treacherous waters shackled & maimed; waded in and out.
Our feet hung over those waters, shark-filled, alligator immersed.

Yet we came to the water;
first navigators, Black skin reflecting in deep blue.
We are the water: fluid, cohesive, unbounded,
    the building blocks of life.

Artist Statement: *I submitted to the magazine's theme of Cultural Memory! Art has been used as a form of resistance throughout history, directly and indirectly. In general and for all intents and purposes, resistance is defined as the act of resisting using some kind of force. For me, Pac-Man symbolizes the ideal non-violent role-playing-game (RPG). Its designer and creator, Toru Iwatani, developed the game to be cute, fun, unique, colorful and accessible to all ages and sexual orientations. It was also designed to be "non-violent." Nowadays, 99 percent of RPGs are designed with some kind of violent imagery, weapons, and scenarios/situations. Hence, my cultural memory relating to acts of resistance using art as it pertains to video games as an idealized RPG using non-violent imagery, story, and designs.*

Pac-Man was definitely a cultural memory for me and most Asians that grew up in the 1980s and early '90s. It was one of the most popular and successful arcade games/role-playing games of all time. The game's object was simple, and the controls were easy to follow, enabling all ages to enjoy and play it. The uniqueness and cuteness of the characters also made the game appealing to both males and females, young and old players alike. Yet, for its inherent simplicity and primitiveness, the game needed a lot of skills, patience, and practice in order for players to master it. At that time, Pac-Man was also considered the most innovative and addictive game, both fun and non-violent. For gamers, developers, and coders, it was a blueprint for things to come. Pac-Man was a universal game changer (pun intended) as it revolutionized arcade games and role-playing games for years to come.

– Val Guevarra

The Games We Play

Artist Statement: *This poem is about cultural memory on the individual and collective level in the face of gaslighting, erasure, and self-doubt.*

–Jess Heard

Poetry Therapy

I write
to survive
the gaslighting

Marks on the wall
gird my truth
counter your denial

I track all
I can recall

Stand against
all these many slights

Stumbling through
shifting quicksands
vacillating winds

My mind
is the surest and steadiest
unsteadiness
within reach

Artist Statement: *I am reaching for connection in this time of isolation. As the pandemic continues, I reach for my outer community, for friends, familiarity, and cultural memory. My resistance right now is giving myself the mission of sketching each follower on my IG account and tagging their name in the sketch/portrait of them. As I do this, I make connections. I give a gift. I do this to be seen and to see from where I am to where they are. During these two winters of a pandemic, I have become weary of the digital world, yet am left with using it to connect and to create. I try to do one drawing a day. I have very few followers. It's not about that for me. This is about practicing my art, setting goals, and giving myself something to do that connects me with others in a way that is enjoyable for me and them. I needed a way to connect online that wasn't about talking or listening. We've been doing a lot of that since last year. I need to feel and to be felt. No words are needed. Much felt. That's my resistance now.*

– Nikki Depriest

Art Therapy and Connection in Isolation

Ashley

1. **Ashley** – "Liberation to me means financial freedom, independence, and peace. It's gaining the ability to shut off my ego and be transparent when I'm alone with myself and in my thoughts. Liberation to me means one day again, feeling safe in the company of another man."

Gabrielle Bonseigneur

2. **Gabrielle Bonseigneur** – "Liberation to me is freeing myself from the limits and beliefs I subscribed to and placed upon myself while navigating through the journeys of life. It feels like the shedding of who society and others tell me I should be, how I should do things, and what choices I should make. It's embracing and speaking my truth, creating a space that allows me to show up in my rawest form daily, and being unapologetic about it. It's me honoring myself and standing in my beliefs and truth, knowing it goes against everything I've been taught and told. I am more than willing and satisfied with disappointing others so that I remain true to myself and free."

Luminisa

3. **Luminisa** – "Liberation has played a huge role in my life. To me, it means to be so free and live in such a way that you encourage and inspire others so that they can be free from anything and anyone that holds them back from being their highest self.

Ty Prophecy

Artist Statement: *The need for a cultural memory is to be a part of the ancestors, the divine points in which we grow as people. Here we see the ocean, the flowing energy. The elements stored below have manifested into their own practices, legends, and times of challenge. To reconstruct a cultural memory is to recreate the medicine and have similar plans to get a similar effect and/or product justified. The ocean is the middle man to the memory that is rebuilt in the hearts of those that seek its overflowing wealth of knowledge and power. Yet we see the memory within the sea as a calm center for the revival of community to begin.*

— Noah Humphrey

My Soul

My soul is the drilling of jackhammers and replays of Nipsey Hussle
My soul has the taste of fresh coffee and the afterburners
    on tricked-out cars
My soul is given the name freedom
The background of my soul comes from a construction site
    on Slauson in South Central LA.

Remembrance of Bussed Down Seats

I remember sitting on a bus seat on a Fresno Metro Bus
I see my job and the school I went to
From school to my sibling's house, then the mall,
    then to my family's house
I see the roaches at night
Cold, cold night, undamaged and stoic bed sheets
Mildew and rust
The smell of complacency
Are what thrives off the page
When the hollow cries that demand an onomatopoeia
Petering out of my wall of debris and financial clutter
You look, you see, what more travel can one soul hold payment
    to the brain?

And the Catholic-Christian
sacrificing a cat as part of his Mary, a Christian deity, reserved
   loosely in a paranoid frenzy body
This one, mad with insanity,
hid the cat to sacrifice him without the consent of the owner and the
   children crying to take him out of that wooden fortress
And like how I rescue the cat, I think the travel that could have sent
   this man to be in a straightjacket
Yet I hold my community peacefully as a bus full of seats on a Sunday
   morning. My bible a compass to self-care and love
Loosely open but still going somewhere

Artist Statement: *This spoken word honors the pain and resilience of the women within my bloodline. It is a reminder of the ancestral trauma that Indigenous and Women of Color carry from colonization and patriarchy. Those wounds get passed down through intergenerational trauma, broken relationships, and self-harm. As has been the case for me. However, this poem is about acknowledging the pain, breaking cycles, and navigating healing by tapping into my ancestors' resilience. It resolves through my present journey as a mother doing the work to raise a strong, sovereign, whole daughter. It offers healing and awakens the divine feminine and warrior within us all.*

– Lauren Ballesteros

This House

The sun slowly sets as she stares,
Worn front steps.
Returning here, her biggest challenge, to this day
It's hard to be present when she found herself away
From this place she used to call
Home.
This house is a time capsule, full of mirrors,
Here salvation lies in a room where a child's cries
They are stacked high in piggy banks of open wounds.
She's a hoarder of memories
Too painful to utter, they clutter her mind,
And formed several disorders.
Starving herself of affection
Binging on insecurity and anxiety,
Purging misguided attempts at perfection.
She made herself a victim to fear-filled vices
Letting ANGER live deep inside
It plots against her, constructing her doom.

After years of hiding it, she realizes she's fed on it
Since her mother's womb, attached to her mother's pain,
ANGER is why she was born purple and blue,
The umbilical cord strangling her breath,

her tears, her
Voice.

The language of silence is in her bloodline
Resilient women whose strength
Is carefully calculated, vanity,
But if you look closer, you'll see
Dark shadows dancing in callous eyes.
Traces of that forgotten girl
Too small to say, "Stop no."
So now she says it too much,
Won't let anyone in
Deeply disturbed by a lover's touch.
It sends shivers; she's triggered, she's mean.

But outside this house, weeds grow,
Those that take advantage of the forgotten girl
That doesn't know; not every legacy is made the same.
Life is a twisted game when you're a descendant of a mother
Land conquered by forced entry
Maimed in the name of victory without consent.
On that day goddesses wailed, the winds howled
As my mothers were forced to bow on their hands and knees –
Birth unwanted seeds on trails of tears
Silenced by our forefathers that labeled her his "property."
But through their cries, they prophesied,
"False kings create false gods to hide.
They keep us divided-fighting a hell within ourselves.
The truth is – it's just a matter of time till we rise,
"Again."

This is where my story begins,
The "forgotten girl" that remembers
I came into this lifetime with a mission
The truth, hidden in every strand of my DNA –
Activated by my intuition.
We, the "forgotten," are like dandelions.

Born out of and into circumstances beyond our control
But from the rubble we still grow-
We inherited much more than our ancestors' pain
Our pollen is potent- a powerful alchemy of equal parts –
Resistance, resilience, hard lessons, and broken dreams
They're counting on you and me to fulfill their one wish
Break the cycle – set them free.

I'm a dandelion mother, watering my seed with intention
My nectar is sweet and sour, and won't let anything disrupt
Stepping into my power, especially me
Rooted in the understanding that my healing
Is directly tied to my daughter's ability
To live in her truth as a sovereign being –
So I speak to her mindfully, nurture her consciously
Constantly challenging myself to give her the best of me
Knowing our time is temporary, but our bond is eternal
She chose this moment to enter my world,
    giving me the strength I need
To confront the harsh realities of a society operating at a low frequency
But we are raising the vibration to levels of divinity
Reigning in goddess energy in the 21st century
With all my mothers beside me,
She is our phoenix rising.

Artist Statement: *This piece aligns with Cultural Memory. Connecting to our own ancestral magic is an act of liberation. When we are deeply rooted, we are nourished by the resilience that is in our DNA. This is magical and it is our destiny.* – Mariana Aq'ab'al Moscoso

You Are The Magic

Artist Statement: *I am the daughter of Abdelkader Daoudi, and my father's side of the family is native to the region of Ain Defla in northwestern Algeria. Algeria is the largest country in Africa, touching the Mediterranean Sea to the north with a geography that is made up of scenic beaches, stunning mountains, dense forests, rich farmlands, and the vast Sahara Desert. Bordered by Morocco, Mauritania, Mali, Niger, Libya and Tunisia, it has always been a conduit and crossroads for travel and trade between west and southern Africa and the Mediterranean. It is an incredibly beautiful and diverse country with a proud history and of course its share of modern-day struggles.*

France occupied Algeria for 132 years. My Algerian ancestors suffered many generations of violence and humiliation at the hands of settler colonialism. My family's farmland and farmhouse was bulldozed and destroyed by French soldiers, and my grandfather and great-uncles were imprisoned and tortured multiple times. My father was eleven years old when Algeria finally won its independence after a bloody, seven-year revolutionary war and I'm often brought to tears thinking of the horrors he must have witnessed as a small child. Generations later, the legacy and trauma of colonization still impacts every single one of our families. There are hidden atrocities being uncovered even now. France has yet to formally apologize for its 132 years of brutal colonization or discuss any kind of reparative action which has been called for by Algerians for decades.

In March of 2021, France was hit by huge dust storms that carried sand all the way across the Mediterranean from the Sahara Desert. It became a news headline and images of rust-colored Saharan dust sprinkled all over French villages started circulating online. It was found that this sand and dust contained abnormally high levels of radiation, remnants of nuclear testing done by the French in the Algerian Sahara during the time of colonization.

France detonated its first atomic bomb called the Gerboise Bleue near the desert oasis of Reggane in southern Algeria in February of 1960. The bomb was four times stronger than the Hiroshima bomb. A second bomb, Gerboise Blanche, was set off a few months later. Public records say that France tested a total of 17 nuclear bombs over many decades, although the extent of the testing in the Sahara is still not fully known as France has yet to declassify many of its colonial records. Many inhabitants of these regions of the Sahara have suffered severe health problems because of the radiation to date.

The Sand Remembers is a digital collage that stitches together and remixes short clips of archival footage from the actual nuclear explosion in 1960 and recent radar imagery of radioactive Saharan sand being blown across the Mediterranean into France and Europe in 2021. The audio accompanying the images is sourced from the soundtrack of the iconic film The Battle of Algiers. *The driving rhythm of the drum and krakeb (metal castanets) overlaid with a chorus of zaghreet (ululations) is found in the final scene of the film where viewers are brought to the precipice of an all out revolution and left with images of a crowd of Algerians pushing forward through dust and smoke waving the Algerian flag and yelling, "tahya Al Djazair!" or "long live Algeria!"*

While I have known about this story for some time, I was moved to create this piece only after living in and learning from people on the other side of the world in the Pacific. While the violence of American colonization here in Hawai'i shows up in slightly different ways than it did for Algerians with France, it is equally as destructive and detrimental to people and the planet. I've been navigating an internal conflict knowing that I'm participating in the continued illegal occupation of the Kingdom of Hawai'i as an American/Algerian settler as someone whose own family dealt with outsiders taking our land, renaming our sacred places, suppressing our culture, and enacting everyday violence and humiliation on our people.

Living in the Pacific has also exposed me to the deplorable history of nuclear testing that happened in this part of the world. Much like their views of the Sahara, both France and the, in this case also the United States, deemed smaller islands of the Pacific disposable, so remote that no one would know or care what kind of devastation happened in the wake of testing of their nuclear bombs.

Well, the Saharan sand remembers, just as the Pacific waters do. Just as the people do, the land and the water will remind us of what we've done and what we've been through, both the pain and the beauty. It will remind us that we must be accountable to each other, that borders don't exist, that everything on earth is connected, and we cannot escape the violence that we enact on each other and the planet. The land and the water can also heal us, just as we can heal it. We're still here, and we still remember.

The Sand Remembers, 2021

To enjoy this multimedia Cultural Remembrance, please scan the QR code:

CHAPTER 2
Accountability

Kolu by David Akeo

The woven hair is substantial and strong. The braids are not free-flowing, but solid. The negative white space indicates snow on Mauna Kea. The Mauna is the body of a wāhine, life herself.

"Everybody against me. Why? Why me? I have not brought violence to you. I have not brought Thug Life to America. I didn't create Thug Life. I diagnosed it". — Tupac Amaru Shakur

Accountability is critical in building a resistance movement. If we are to erect a whole, functioning, and inclusive community, everyone must be honored. In the context of our resistance, accountability ensures the well-being of the individual and collective, the land that nourishes us, and the systems, infrastructures, and resources that support functioning, just societies. Accountability in the context of our resistance and liberation requires the dissolution of hegemonic processes. We must call out false narratives, unearned privileges, and the status quo. We must be brave enough to know and understand our stories and their stories, too, with depth and clarity.

Accountability is a commitment to the inherent self-determination and sovereignty of all peoples. And, as Tupac advised, we must welcome the truth, however ugly and regrettable, shocking or new. Ultimately, accountability asks us to bear witness to the world we live in now, so we may imagine a radically different future. Accountability allows us to support the possibility and continuation of a functioning society for everyone. Accountability is not a fancy word for punishment. It is not a chore, but a privilege. Accountability is love and love is life.

Dr. Manu Meyer, a Hawaiian scholar and epistemologist, conceptualizes collective accountability in the Hawaiian worldview as a requisite for survival. Meyers says, "We mutually evolve, or don't, simultaneously." In her book *Ho'oulu: Our Time Of Becoming*, Meyer expands on the concept of kuleana (accountability), a concept not too dissimilar from the idea of accountability we bring to mind here. Meyer says of kuleana:

> Understanding our kuleana develops our human potential because it ties us to our function and our function ties us to our people. It is this sequence because we value what we must do in order to continue to steward our language, our oceans, our lands. We must because we have that responsibility. Knowing who we are, then, becomes a prerequisite to know how best we can serve (p. 13).

The following stories ask us to bear witness and be accountable to old and new ways of being. They call to account our responsibility to self and others and direct our attention to the lived experiences of our authors and artists.

Artist Statement: *I wrote this poem during the summer of 2021 when masses of people began to gather in protest against the state of Hawai'i-mandated vaccination. Seeing all of the American flags in the streets of Waikiki was very triggering as a kanaka 'ōiwi wahine. Seeing my own Hawaiian people holding signs that erased our Black 'ohana was also very triggering to me as a Black Womxn.*

To me, this poem is a call that we are connected and therefore need to be accountable to one another. Standing in solidarity and not in alignment with the systems and people that try to keep us oppressed.

– Joshlyn Noga

Erasure

Don't let them erase us, Hawaiian.

Koko 'ole out in the streets
chanting,
I kū maumau.

While kānaka waving signs that say,
"Hawaiian Lives Matter."

Stop erasing folxs!

Stealing from the movements
of other people.

That's that mentality,

that gotta go.

Caught slipping
Missing the rats
Gnawing through the walls

That's the haoles.
If you didn't know.

Every day I understand
a little more.

Why our kūpuna decided

Cook had to go.

Sick of seeing
haoles waving their American flags.

No different than the time,
Dole conspired and stole.

Reinforcing the disrespect
like when our Queen
was illegally
Overthrown.

Erasure!

Artist Statement: *'Āhui hala is the fragrant fruit that grows on the pūhala tree (pandanus). When ripe, the 'āhui hala turns a vibrant yellow, orange, or red color. Accompanying these colors is a sweet citrus scent. Our kupuna (ancestors) cherished the 'āhui hala's beauty and fragrance. An ōlelo no'eau (Hawaiian proverb) speaks to the beauty of this fruit, "A'ohe hala 'ula i ka pō" which means no hala fruit shows its color in the darkness of night. The ōlelo no'eau suggests that beauty must be seen to be enjoyed. Āhui Hala is a reminder to think about the aloha our ancestors had for 'āina (land) and as descendants, we must continue to cultivate that pilina (relationship) today.*

– Pūlama Long

Ahuihala

Pūlama Long

Artist Statement: *Accountability is doing the healing as it's instructed, from the past, and not to harm like the methods done by leaders before, but to heal. As I march, I understand that my actions create a movement. Her life is not in vain and from my walk and my activism I hold accountability for those who see this sign to say her name and for the community to gaze at my sign with the knowledge that she won't be erased. We cannot make haste with those treated with injustice lest we forget who we are as human beings. To be spiritual is to engage in a spiritual struggle.*

To be a healer you also have to enact on the injustice faced within your world. –Noah Humphrey

My Own Wallowing Words

I promise that the words I do not yet have

will form under the mouths of oppressed citizens in a governing state

I promise that the words I do not have will be buried in the ocean
along with my ancestors

I promise that the words I do not have will be embedded
like piko on the land of Mauna Kea

for what is sacrality?

I promise that the words I do not have will be fluffed with the words
of inflation and generational trauma like cotton candy

I need to say that it's sugary and sweet

I need to say that the ocean will hear the undead cries for liberation

I need to say that life in the sacred land will be healing

And the tyrannies you swallow day by day like foreign sand
on a forbidden island paradise

creates their own sickening silence

Who will falter like the rose that lies in the promising lands

and attempt to make your own until you sicken and die of them,
still in silence?

I promise that the sassy applauding root you called to rut
will be a wholesale of absorbed energy that will pin the
damp constructs of capitalism under its feet

And I promise that the private tense apparels that are fashioned
from the individual marauders that rampant ill-fated parks
intervened to duck cheap listeners

Ignore the deafening obscene voices called a promise

And then, do you still intend to tell me my job is done?

Kick Rocks

Artist Statement: *This essay addresses all themes of resistance: Accountability, Cultural Memory, Countering Hegemony, and Resisting False Binaries. However, this essay is first and foremost about accountability. This is a loving request for Black women to REST. Rest is resistance.* – Amy Benson

The word REST is in Resistance

Naija no dey carry last. As a first-generation Nigerian American, the significance of community continuously manifests throughout the culture in familial, tribal, and spiritual ways. Within that, there is culturally immense pressure to be successful. Not only are you subject to cultural expectations, but you are also subject to societal expectations of the country in which you were born. In my case, the United States of America. Black women of all ethnicities are constantly navigating life with so many imposed expectations and criticism of how we should express ourselves, what we should feel, what we should wear, how much success we should achieve without making others feel insecure, how we should shrink ourselves, what age we should be married by, how much labor we should extend freely, and the list goes on.

There are universal expectations that our value is attached to our bodies, how much struggle we can endure, or how much we can do for other people even if that means putting ourselves last. Nah. I am not subscribing to ideologies surrounded by expectations of Black women being superheroes to the world and not needing rest. Our resilience should not be used as a cognitive dissonance crutch for people that insist on dumping their foolery on us just because we can "handle" it.

I am the youngest of my mother's five children. I grew up in different cities in Alabama, a place known to be the poster of what "traditional racism" in America looks like. We lived in low-income public housing for most of my childhood and adolescence. However, the community was still present in those challenging environments. Community, in so many ways, is a requirement for survival for Black folk. Drugs and crime surrounded me, but also around hard-working Black families.

Although I was immersed in Black American culture socially and environmentally, when I walked into my home, there was a strong presence of Nigerian culture. The distinctive smell of stockfish, music playing by Osadebe, Sunny Ade, Fela Kuti, and my mother's very dramatic Igbo accent are tattooed on the fabric of my upbringing.

My mother grew up during the Biafran war in Nigeria and was 15 when it began. Many Igbo people believe the correct name should be the Biafran Genocide. Many of her friends and family were killed during that time. Ironically, the war ended on her 18th birthday, January 15, 1970. According to my mother, she actually never connected the dots of it being her birthday because, at that time, there were no birthday celebrations. Many people did not even know what date they were born on. However, she does remember vividly when she learned of the news the war had ended.

My father, a Yoruba man, was part of the Nigerian military. He had joined towards the end of the Biafran war like many young boys and men did. He met my mother in 1977, and they were married the same year in Nigeria. My parents arrived in the United States in 1983 and were to be in the U.S. temporarily for my father's work and his schooling. After completing his assignments in May 1987, he returned to Nigeria as scheduled. My mother was pregnant with me at that time. I was born three months after my father's departure. Initially, we were to reunite with my father in Nigeria. However, she decided to stay in America permanently. Divorce soon followed, and we never returned to Nigeria as initially planned.

My first visit to Nigeria was during my father's burial in 2011. My mother worked several jobs while earning her college degrees. She raised five of us on her own in a country foreign to her. I have vague memories of my mother resting. Even as a kid, my mom would not let us sleep in on the weekends. Her thick accent echoed throughout the house, "Amy, wake up. It's time to do real cleanup today." LOL. She taught us many things like resilience and hard work, but resting was not one of them.

We were the only Nigerians in my neighborhood, and all my friends that I saw regularly were mostly Black Americans. My siblings and I were members of a Nigerian society, and my mother would bring us to their hosted functions and activities. Although I did not live around any of those Nigerians I knew from society, it allowed me to meet other Nigerian kids my age. In the early 1990s, it was not "cool" to be Nigerian in the inner-city projects or ghettos. There was a huge disconnect, and that was hard to understand as a child. I began learning Black American literature, music, and truly all things representing Black culture. I remember feeling not Nigerian enough for Nigerians and too African for Americans. This was conflicting as a child because we were all Black in my head. As I began to learn more, I became more proud of being Nigerian-American.

I am a Black Nigerian American queer woman, and all those pieces of me are important. Integrating my Nigerian upbringing with Black American culture metaphorically represents one of my intentions with the Black Bazaar HNL. I created Black Bazaar HNL as a social organization and community connecting Black people in Hawai'i through wellness, joy, creativity, culture, entertainment, economics, and more. It's a reflection of several identities within the wide spectrum of Blackness. I wanted to interconnect the Black civilian and Black military communities here in Hawai'i, and together we could embrace all the pieces of our identities that connect us, even in the Pacific.

With Hawai'i's population being less than 4% Black, no designated districts serve as a representation of Black culture. When I arrived here eight years ago, there were no areas besides military installations that you knew for certain Black people would be. Relocating from Atlanta to Honolulu, I quickly asked myself, "Wait a minute! Like, where are all the Black folks?!" It's not that Hawai'i doesn't have a rich Black history because she does. However, over the years, the visibility of Blackness has increased tremendously, and I think organizations like Black Bazaar HNL are just one of the many reasons that contribute to it.

In March 2020, Black Bazaar HNL hosted our first Penthouse Pop-Up Event to support small Black business owners and creatives on the island. It was a bazaar of multiple vendors selling items ranging from clothing to haircare products. There was live entertainment, food prepared by chefs, and activities for attendees to participate in while they shopped. Beautiful Black faces freely navigating through three levels of vendors and activities while exuding joy and supporting one another was a very special feeling. I remember being extremely present. One week later, the pandemic hit, and our calendar of in person events were canceled one after another. That was the last time many of us would see one another until the Black Bazaar Juneteenth Cookout.

My focus shifted to curating the community virtually by providing free resources such as live talks with clinical psychologists, wellness experts, financial advisors, etc. We also supported small business owners, doing giveaways, having talent shows, games, safe spaces for dialogue, and other community-building activities. I was very intentional about cultivating Black joy in these spaces. Over the next few months, our on-island virtual community grew exponentially, the social engagement was high, unapologetic, Black, and safe.

Simultaneously, as the community I was birthing began blossoming, every other area of my life began deteriorating. With the loss of my salaried consulting position in 2020, the height of civil unrest with the murders of Ahmaud Arbery, Breonna Taylor, and George Floyd, and isolation left me completely drained. My lifestyle concierge company, Planes and Champagne, was severely financially impacted by the decrease in travel, safety concerns around Covid, on-island restrictions, and shutdowns. Neither Planes and Champagne nor Black Bazaar HNL received any funding during this pandemic. I was still so committed to serving this community in ways that I could. The pandemic has challenged me mentally, financially, and spiritually. Although my therapist did help me navigate some of the challenges I was facing internally, I still felt like a failure. I felt like everything that I had worked for had dissipated. Despite creating an amazing community, I felt inadequate and struggled with self-doubt.

Healing while Black is already difficult enough; lord have mercy to do it in a pandemic. It exasperated existing traumas, anxiety, and depression; for some, the pandemic activated it. The importance of community became even more critical in the ways those anxieties were manifesting for people. I continued to pour myself into community and relationships. In hindsight, it was hypocritical of me to encourage radical self-care and curate spaces for people to prioritize their mental and spiritual health while neglecting my own. But I had to keep going. I kept telling myself, "Power through." I did just that until I couldn't any more.

"Rest is Reparations"

In the summer of 2021, I hit a mental and physical wall, and it was then I began to rest, restore, and replenish. I began setting healthy boundaries, prioritizing my mental and spiritual health, and removing things that did not serve me in positive ways to free up some bandwidth that I could allocate to my journey of healing. I stopped looking at things that had gone wrong and started focusing on things that had gone right. Letting go of the responsibility of continuously showing up and producing something that will last felt liberating. I'm that "strong" friend; many times, people do not know what we do and feel in the dark. We are not exempt from life's challenges. Life be life-ing! On my mirror, I wrote, "It's ok to rest, sis." It served as a reminder and helped me remove the guilt around resting. Resting is resistance. Resting is revolutionary.

"Starting over isn't starting from scratch."

The pandemic has taught me that starting over means a chance to have a new perspective. Starting over means you now have the experience you didn't have before. Starting over means the lessons you learned may not need to be learned again. Starting over means returning to the drawing board with new concepts, creativity, and compassion. Starting over means rearranging not necessarily removing. Starting over means being able to identify when you need rest. I've healed and grown so much in unimaginable ways. This community evolved so much together. If there is one takeaway I'd like for anyone reading this to remember, it is that resting should not be a luxury, especially for Black women. Resting is a requirement. Resting is self-care. Resting is part of our overall wellness. We need it, deserve it, and should not feel guilty for it. So, rest up, sis, then take up space.

Artist Statement: *This piece speaks to cultural memory and account-ability in that it addresses how misogyny affects us on an interpersonal level.* – Alejandra Alexander

*Content warning: This piece shares the author's experience with rape and abuse.

Don't Call Me Daddy

WAINANI PAIKAI

There's a picture of you on my altar
holding hands with my Mother
sometime before I was born,
I presume.
You can't see the predation in this polaroid of you two.
You can't see that she is a child and you are eleven years her senior.
I can see it though.
Whenever a new lover asks me to call her daddy
 whilst we're panting over each other,
I remember being 14 and the grown-ass man who looked like you
     but wasn't
panting on top of me in the back seat of his car
where he had to take out his child's car seat before he
     raped me there.
He asked me to call him daddy while he did it.
I can see you.
I'm not sure why this picture is on my altar to be honest.
You aren't really dead.
You're alive somewhere in Texas.
Growing old
Growing old
Asshole
"Cassanova"
My mother is still alive, too,
recovering from you.
From the cacophony of yous that she's endured for too much of her
     life.
She's alive,
reclaiming her sense of safety.
The child she was in that Polaroid is long dead, though.
Sometimes I get fleeting glimpses of her forgetting to be afraid.
Stealing joy from her trauma.
But still when I press my weight on a woman,
lick her neck, and she wetly whispers "daddy,"
I see you
and all the blood drains from my clit

nestled atop my silicone dick
and I have to remind myself,
out loud,
to her, that I'm not her daddy.
I'm not my daddy.
This dick isn't real, and that's my favorite thing about it.
I'm not you, daddy.
It may be the mitote talking, but I'm certain
I'm so much better than you.

– Alejandra Alexander

Artist statement: *This poem was written as a form of accountability to remind me of my kuleana to others and me. I'm reminded each day that our communities are rooted in resistance, and just as those before have poured into me, I hope to do the same for others. If you're reading this, I hope you feel your ancestors' cultural memory reminding you of your generational strength.*

– Kealohilani Minami

Commitments of Kuleana

For my inner light
i am ʻāina
the land that feeds & provides in abundance
knowing i am in a reciprocal relationship
our intimacy is sealed with love poems
about the ways you've held me & nourished life
in the dead of night,

For my kūpuna
i am a lei
woven with your dreams & intentions
bound together with unbreakable chords
conceived in a space somewhere between lepo & pō
may i honor you & the ancestral memories
you've left for me rooted in my naʻau
i'm learning to decolonize my tongue so i may
hear your voice clearer
allowing me to follow in your legacy,

For my mana māhū ʻohana
i am wai
constantly shifting, rising, flowing
always without fail dedicated to sharing ke ola
our waters met & merged for a reason
letting me know we aren't separate
because we're fundamentally, anatomically the same
as mist enveloping the space around us

one minute there, the next gone like lilinoe
with gentle reminders of aloha,

For my trauma
i am a mele
whispering sweet melodies
composing lullabies to soothe my inner demons
when they beg for me to love them
mele that holds you when your chest is so tight
you cannot feel anything else
but the harmonies in one ear and out the other,

For my comrades
i am ea
sharing life for our collective sovereignty
may we remember our deep rooted intricacies
hold space in tender aloha
while we sing
e aloha e
     e aloha e
standing face to face with those who refuse
our humanity, this mele keeps us in kapu aloha
our hands grip tighter woven arm to arm
through hell so we may get
a sweet taste of freedom,
For the youth in my community
i am a basket
i can only hope to carry your aspirations & tears
in return share my harvest of each passing season
i prepare you for deep learning & unlearning
to overcome lies rooted in colonialism
forcefully shoved down our throat until we
no longer remember the way our ancestors breathed life into us
let me share my hā with you
pressed forehead to forehead
may these words leave an imprint in your mind
the way Kumu Haunani-Kay Trask

the way Kumu Teresia Teaiwa
shared with us
holding us in their baskets of resilience
teaching through their words & actions
what it means to move in alignment with what's pono,

When i wove this basket
i didn't know it could carry the weight of generations
but you've shown me the depth we can grow
of just how much i can carry in my harvest
and so, like those before me
i will stay here
weaving baskets of resilience
to carry our keiki in.

Artist Statement: *This poem is about accountability and the differ-ence between apologies and authentic reparations, restoration, and repair.*

– Jess Heard

Apologies

Your apology is like
a land acknowledgement

A carefully crafted party line
intended to convey awareness
and sincerity
to smooth discontent
while changing nothing

Words and gestures
Without steps to repair the harm

And if I don't give you credit
for uttering the acknowledgment

If I do not graciously submit
that your apology suffices

Am I ungrateful and difficult?
Or righteous and justified?

Perhaps I recall
a different history than you

Are we standing
face-to-face?

Or back-to-back?
Land back.

Artist Statement: *This poem addresses the false binary of "innocent" white people (e.g., liberal/progressive) and "ignorant" white people. It holds both accountable for the destruction their active bigotry and passive performative acts bring to people of the global majority, practically and psychically.*

– Jess Heard

The Mirage

It is not the fault
of the mirror
that they do not like
their reflection

They shatter it anyway

This is US
Fractured
Bitterly divided
Codependent

Innocence blames ignorance

Yet there is neither
innocence nor ignorance
in stolen land and lives

They see what they want to see
a mirage all the same

Healing can come only
from truth and reconciliation
There is no common ground
in moral equivalence
no reconciliation
without truth

The innocent and the ignorant
must listen and follow
those of us born witness to

held hostage by
their whiteness

We who have been consigned
the burden of holding their mirror
tire of these dramatic performances

They shatter the mirror
again and again
but cannot outrun our conscience
only theirs

CHAPTER 3
Countering Hegemony

Kahi 2 by David Akeo

Countering hegemony is all about flipping the script.

You did not seriously think that a Hobbit could contend with the will of Sauron? There are none who can. Against the power of Mordor, there can be no victory. We must join with him, Gandalf. We must join with Sauron. It would be wise, my friend.
—The Lord of the Rings: The Fellowship of the Ring *(film version)*

Hegemony's control over the global political, economic, and cultural realms has given rise to a multitude of injustices, including the slave trade, redlining, US-backed coups in Latin America, the illegal occupation of sovereign nations, and numerous other forms of exploitation. Hegemony encompasses everything from the pervasive influence of corporations like McDonald's to slave wages, unmanageable student loans, medical debt, and the looming threat of global warming. Hegemony imposes distorted beliefs such as "White is right," elevating figures like Donald Trump as idols, and promoting the notion that capitalism is the sole viable option. Cultural hegemony reinforces damaging notions that a woman's ultimate objective is to secure a male partner for salvation, and it also upholds restrictive beauty standards that predominantly favor whiteness and a particular body type.

Hegemony's ultimate objective is to assimilate, dominate, or eliminate until it achieves absolute power over every facet of existence—individuals, ideas, places, and ways of being. The endgame is the establishment of a single ruler, a single power, and a single way of life. This can be likened to Sauron's all-seeing eye in *The Lord of the Rings*, symbolizing hegemonic control and assimilation. Much like the eye's omnipresence, hegemony's influence is ever-present, even when we are alone. It coerces us, making us feel like marionettes, manipulated to conform in ways that betray our true selves.

Throughout my life, I've grappled with this all-seeing eye. I've felt compelled to conform to societal expectations, often at the expense of my authentic identity. The eye dictated how I should present myself, encouraging shame in my natural appearance. It pushed me towards embodying the white aesthetic. Any attempt to question its grip was discouraged and considered dangerous. Defiance meant risking my safety. I couldn't conceal my brown skin or female identity, but I attempted to emulate white beauty standards, speaking softly and suppressing questions that challenged the status quo.

I did all this because hegemonic norms, whether implicit or explicit, have been drilled into our minds as the norm, making anything outside them seem inferior and abnormal. I unwittingly consented to the dominance of white supremacy, fearing the consequences of resisting what society deemed "common sense." Even the briefest online search reveals the harsh penalties those who defy this hegemonic power face.

According to Italian Marxist philosopher Antonio Gramsci, hegemony is wielded through coercion and unconscious consent, often cultivated through education and ideology. We're often unaware of this indoctrination, and that's by design. Whether through textbooks, memes, or legal systems, hegemonic forces shape our beliefs. The values unique to the dominant group become seen as universal, while other perspectives are marginalized.

European expansion laid the groundwork for white cultural hegemony, which strives to eliminate opposing cultures' sovereignty. In his insightful analysis, scholar David Allen sheds light on the pervasive influence of dominant ideologies in structuring societal hierarchies. His work examines how these ideologies place whiteness at the apex, inherently marginalizing those who do not fit into the categories of white, heterosexual, or male. Allen's research offers a compelling critique of how these ingrained societal structures rationalize and perpetuate the subjugation of diverse identities in support of cultural hegemony.

In response to this hegemonic control, the following works offer counter-narratives that challenge the prevailing norms. These courageous artists and authors provide alternative perspectives, encouraging us to reconsider the world through new lenses. These voices stand against powers that have suppressed sovereign lands, diverse identities, and unique stories. They reclaim the power that was unjustly taken away.

Artist Statement: *My two submissions (an Untitled poetry piece and a mixed media collage entitled Aloha ʻĀina) are deeply rooted in resistance. This is my preferred form of healing as a Black Hawaiian Chinese Filipina First Nation mother forced to reside in amerikkka. Resistance is a conscious choice I make in my everyday battle against oppression. I believe in the bravery of speaking up to release hidden pain to heal ancestral wounds. Both of my pieces speak directly to this necessary shift.* – Malia Connor

Aloha ʻĀina

Untitled

I've been told that I need to write more love poems
except love can also look like struggle
feel like hopelessness
veiled behind well-to-do gestures
while immersed in the violence of colonialism.

I've been told that I need to practice more "aloha"
that I sound too Black to be Hawaiian
look too Hawaiian to be Black
but that's what happens when you normalize whiteness
using their reality to see.

I've been told that I need to write more love poems
except hatred focuses on the melanated
I fiercely protect my Tribe
by always challenging patriarchal racism
because "aloha" also means goodbye.

I've been asked why Black Lives Matter in Hawai'i
and after recovering from my initial shock
I tenderly try to reeducate the false narratives
force-fed since 1893
and all I ask from white men is to cease speaking indefinitely.

I've been told that I need to write more love poems
using settler language, which I mindfully refuse
instead, I take up space
fist clenched, raised high
defiant in my golden sage years as a student.

I've been told what I need
but love poems? that is all I ever write
dropping truth serums while delightfully
ignoring your entitled discomfort
preferring to watch a Nation of Warriors RISE!

Artist Statement: *Everyone can build as a healer, but not all can deconstruct their trauma. No matter your identity, we all work toward healing the land. And yet how to build a world where we can understand the power we do have? There is joy in creating. There is anger in destruction. To experience the bountifulness of the lessons given to the land, we must introduce ourselves back to the nature that forged us. As we solidify our being, demonstrate our inner soul of wellness via self-care, and expand community service allying with the greater good, we can break those structures that threaten to counter our claims to the healing which we effortlessly use for strength and compassion for all.*

— Noah Humphrey

Baby's/Myeni's Eulogy

Are you ready to get rid of the main attraction?
The soul is the main valve to the heart's satisfaction
Therapy sessions don't cover what's always next
And the innocent heads that lay right to Westernized necks
That had no names to say that I'm okay
No brain that can aim in the same way

I am intent with the rhymes,
I moved in my body to be steady
And if that gun didn't shoot ten times,
would my soul really be ready
I am not in the mood for this,
describing happy homes underneath bandages
The fear became the never-ending bandage
of imperialism
Dig a hole and put a beet in it,
dig a soul deeper where the racist tweet
can't hear it
Burning smoke from the bullet holes
encased in the barrages of kids that have never seen
propagation and the legislation
the tourism schemes have been accurately learned

And where can we see these tragedies
where we see these wars encased in the souls
that never called me by by name

Iremamber, Iremamber, Iremamber
Lindani, Lindani, Lindani

Too many times, we screamed for the attractions
that never settled hell on its doorstep
I want to know the spirit and the government
that calls the lies and listening factors
that could never repair the rooms or the wombs
of the broken families entrenched in systems
where the spam spoils, the language is taken,
the islands are barraged and barricaded away
from the true ancestors, where half of the population
arrive on Turtle Island unaware that by adapting
the cable that is visible becomes a submerger
of their greatest fears and unbridles the warping tears
that fetters the world of the colonizer unable to accustom
their own thoughts to the systems
that valued family, correction, agriculture, peace,
and equitable ways in which the ones
that are sanctioned for battle are not given
the same times the same tithes nor the same lies
that implies that the injustice system is just for show
And no Moana, no ABC, no Ige, no colonizers,
no telescopes, no plastic aloha can ever let that go.

America

Allison Jacobs

The situation was stacked against us from the start. It was rooted in yesterday, and its seeds were sown in bygone times – the time when we were kidnapped and brutalized and forced to do unspeakable acts.

It was nourished and rocked to sleep by a lullaby made of the oppressor's prayers for an economy of free labor, and these prayers, this religion, was used against us.

It was nourished and grew stronger and more dangerous by the false accusations and tears of women with no melanin.

It bullied its way into an established culture like a cuckoo, laying its eggs into another bird's nest to be hatched and fed, stealing their nourishment.

Its roots grabbed onto stolen land with a death grip, and it sprouted into a full-grown weed, a dandelion head whose seeds spread on the wind, far and wide like tiny white parachutes spreading the spores of white supremacy and racism.

Its form disguised itself like a chameleon, adapting to the color of the times. The plantation overlords and masters morphed into prison guards and wardens.

We have no idea what the threat looks like, but we know.

Artist Statement: *This print is inspired by the Seeds of Hope project, which centers Indigenous practices, aloha ʻāina, and popular education. Some of the first things we planted as part of the project were the three sisters: beans, corn, and squash. The three sisters come from the cultural wisdom of Native peoples of Turtle Island and are planted together to sustain and support each other as they grow. From such small seeds, will grow plants that nourish one another and eventually our neighborhood. This print is dedicated to all of those who are courageous enough to continue planting seeds of hope in the face of often overwhelming oppression.* – Cassandra Chee

Seeding Solidarity

A Single Braid of Rice

Ahmad Selim Aboagye Xallen

A single braid of rice
Is all you might have been able to bring with you
When they took you
Woven in when the warriors didn't come back
In anticipation
In preparation
A single braid of rice
Is all you had time for
When they moved you
Across woodland and forest
River and lake
Lagoon and ocean
From coast to coast
Did you cry out?
At what point did you unbraid your hair
A single braid of rice
If at all
Did you count the seeds on your head, in your head?
Did you count them like the heads of children
With a hope that they would be planted and nurtured?
Or were you against the idea of counting heads, unlike the monsters
    who counted yours
Who counted everything
Heads
Bodies
Men
Women
Children
Acres
Profit
But somehow never counted the people they enslaved
A single braid of rice

is what you brought with you
Along with your heart
Your soul
Your songs
Your dance
Your language
Your humanity
To a land being overtaken by people who sought to take it all

Mi Enemigo

Gabriel Verduzco

I knew from an early age that I had an enemy.
It started long before America ever had borders,
It began when colonizers
ripped native babies from their mothers. From that day I had hate in me.

It wasn't always a hate thing, originally.
Once proud warriors and healers now turned killers and drug dealers.
I knew from an early age that I had enemies.

Nice white teachers who stamped me with the wax seal of criminality
because of my name. Bitch, I survived slavery and genocide,
    and you call me savage! Go figure.
From that day, I had hate in me.

I am the product of ocēlōtl and revolutionaries, the bearer
    of unparalleled bravery.
You can't ever rename me. I'm as endemic as peyote and sweetgrass;
    my skin is copper.
Like clay and hair like spun ebony silk. I knew from a young age
    that I had enemies.

Because I am the son of chingonas, who silently stuffed tears and abuse
    into each ovary.
Inheriting heartbreak before I was ever born, knowing courage and
    strength even before
losing the umbilical cord. Now I wonder, why do I have hate in me?

I am Mēxíhcatl. What's in the mirror doesn't resemble a Hispanic
    or Latino.
I am a ceremony.
Of love and acceptance. Pain and beauty in one.
It was true that I knew from an early age that I had enemies.
But today, I no longer have hate in me.

Artist Statement: *My art centers my stories and perspectives as an Indigenous Chamoru woman told through traditional legends, motifs, and aesthetics brought into a modern context. Themes that are rooted in my pieces include womanhood, ancestral knowledge, spiritual healing, and resistance to colonialism. The intention behind these pieces is to show that my people and all Indigenous peoples are still here and still fighting; remembering ancestral teachings and stories is central to our healing individually and as a community; and that there is beauty in unapologetically embracing our healing and existence. Overall, I use my artwork to connect to my ancestors and homeland as well as practice storytelling and relationality with my community.*

– Gillian Dueñas

Hånom yo'åmte | Healing waters

Manggagaige ha' ham guini | We're Still Here

I Kåten Kulo' | The Call of the Conch

Artist Statement: *My life is not my own. Every day I am in debt to someone, to some obligation, to intangible and tangible forces that demand my money, labor, time, vital energy, dreams, and breath. I forget that I do have moments, however fleeting, that belongs to me. In those moments, even if that moment is just one breath, I can connect to my eternal creator and the life force that birthed me. That moment is reason enough to sing and celebrate. For now, I have won. For now, I am alive and that, I imagine, disappoints the game master who had anticipated my death long ago.*

This poem was inspired by a day at the beach with my girlfriends. We decided to take selfies, feel pretty, and sing each other's praises even as the all-seeing eye dared to call us unworthy. – Luanna Peterson

How to Play the Game and Win

When no one is watching.
When no one is paying.
When no one is swiping.
We play and sway and slay.
We are not here to keep score.
All things the Game abhors.

We are singing bodies, singing
singing on high what our bodies
cannot deny:
We are so dang fly!

I sing a song for these sexy limbs, sexy hips,
sexy joints, sexy mind, sexy heart and
my sexy caramel skin that kisses the fiery sun
the salty air and fertile water
and says, Thank You.

I sing a song for my hips that move and dip.
A song for my mind and heart that transmits,
absorbs and reflects the beauty that is
below, above, and around me.

She's a beauty.

I sing so my living temporal Blackness
mirrors my Creator
in shape, form, and function.

I sing to also scare the Game away.

Some nights, many nights,
the Game takes hold
just as the pen hits the paper,
just as the vision takes form,
just as I'm about to look in the mirror.
It pushes me off the horizon
And then, I am lost.
I don't know how I got there. I'm running
around empty tables, jumping over sinkholes,

slamming against closed doors.

My nightmares are born from the
the fear of the Game
If I lose the Game,
I may starve or die or die alone.

The unopened envelope, the lease, the debt, the rejection.
an ever-present threat.
Play the Game or die, I'm told.

I look at Marie's photos of me
The ones she took when the Game was not looking.
Goofy and awkward. In love and remembering.
This is Why We Sing.

I sing on high, a praise song.
For this my time above, for
this greatest of mysteries,
for this brief moment.
One blink, a breath, one inhale, one exhale.
I sing on high, a praise song.

I sing in this one moment
because, in the next moment, it's gone.
It's Black. Forever. Maybe. We don't know.

I will sing of a dream eternal.
I will sing of a dream beyond the grave,
beyond the Game
with these words.

This song, my moment.
This song, my dream.
This song, my endless life.

Artist Statement: *Every day you hear from non-Black people that we just need not to run away; we need not be aggressive. We need to just listen to what is being said, and we will go home with our lives, yet every officer that does the killing always says that they fear for their lives and are scared, no matter how we act. They were scared and yet they were in a position of power. How do you expect me to sit here and not be scared, but it's okay that someone in a power position can be scared of me or my friends because we are Black? Non-Black people will never understand what we go through, no matter how much they see or hear. It's like talking to the wall, but they'll still hear me scream.*
– Breena Thompson

Proud to be an American

Where at least I can be free
To see folks that look like me
Die endlessly
To hear again and again that we just need to
stay quiet and listen to the damn police

CHAPTER 4
Resisting False Binaries

Kahi by David Akeo

Kahi also means to press or comb, as in long hairs or fibers. As you look at this image, it becomes many different things; it is an illusion. Resisting false binaries is having the ability to decipher illusion from reality.

And all my love to you who preserve the mysteries. Whom the empire of binaries will never define. All of you who love with a depth beyond recognition, nurturing freedom over understandability, valuing life as so much more important than simple comprehension. Thank you. Thank you for loving me without even knowing what on Earth I am"

–Alexis Pauline Gumbs, Undrowned.

Hegemony not only desires absolute power over people and places, but it also seeks to define the boundaries of our imagination and language and the extent of human possibility. In the long run, brute physical force is only effective in maintaining submission for so long. Hegemony limits our ideas and dims our vision so that we arrive at simple but false conclusions. "They are poor because they are _____ and not_____." "If only they would act more like _____, then their lives would be so much better/normal/acceptable." All the while, the arbiters of truth commit the most heinous crimes against humanity, unnoticed and unscathed.

In this land of either-or, locating ourselves at the extreme ends of a spectrum of identity and experience is permissible but nowhere in between. In the fixed imagination of false binaries, we are defined not by the fullness, fluidity, and complexities of our lived experiences but by the violent rendering of an either-or discourse that seeks only to benefit the dominant group. We are defined only in contrast to *not having* the traits of the *other*, whoever the other may be. I am this because I am not that. You are this because you are not that/me/he/she/gay/straight/American/poor/rich/tall/short/able/disabled/light/dark/tall/short/pretty/ugly/fat/skinny/Black/white/brown/Asian/Middle Eastern/Muslim/Christian/old/young/boy/girl/smart/dumb/influencer/follower/third world/first world, you get the idea.

I am a light-skinned, mixed-race, Black, heterosexual, cisgender, poor, single mother raised in Hawai'i. Let's say you, the reader, are also a mother. Does this shared aspect of our identities mean you know my story? Can you truly understand my needs as a mother, the needs of my family, or the challenges my family and ancestors have faced? How have my location, education, race, and sexuality influenced my experience as a mother? And what about your story – the lives, systems, and narratives that have shaped your journey in motherhood? Our paths may converge at motherhood but then diverge in every other aspect. That's perfectly fine. What matters most is our effort to understand each other – not based on preconceived notions or a narrow spectrum of experiences, but through a genuine exchange of our lived stories..

What happens when we don't listen, observe, and respond appropriately to the truth of our lived experiences?

In the 1970s and 1980s, Black feminist scholar-activists such as Barbara Smith of the Combahee River Collective and law professor Kimberlé Crenshaw developed theoretical frameworks to help us understand how we experience marginalization by either-or discourses (Smith). These trailblazers reminded us that feminism is not one size fits all. For example, they said that a woman lives at the intersection of an overlapping system of oppression and privilege. A woman who is white, straight, wealthy, and able-bodied will have lived experiences and opportunities to access power that are much different than a woman who is Black, Lesbian, neurodivergent and experiencing poverty, for example. Though two women share a common gender identity and may have shared lived experiences, their lives diverge where class, race, and sexuality meet. If we fail to acknowledge the complexity of our lived experiences, we are doomed to live in a world of make-believe.

Moreover, when we seek solutions to societal challenges, we will always come up against a wall if our solutions do not reflect the reality of people's lives. This may benefit a select few, as it supports the continuation of their privilege and power. A failure to reckon with the complexity and nuance of our lived experiences will mean that we will forever exist in a nightmare that perpetually reinforces marginalization and limits the full realization of our human potential.

Our human potential is hindered only by the limits we place on our imagination and our ability to embrace and love the unknown. The following stories may be new to you, and the ideas and lived experiences may be foreign and make you feel uncomfortable. Lean into it. Listen and embrace the message and the messenger, even when both defy your comprehension.

Artist Statement: *'Resisting False Binaries' has been embedded in my spirit for years. Through community and self-assessment, I have been gifted with finding the language to communicate this resistance. The idea that everything on this planet, including the social constructs we create, must be immediately placed into a dichotomy, an either-or, is harmful. Unlearning my attachment to gender, the language about gender, and its performance, and learning to understand that I don't have to attach myself to any of that, has been healing. I've found healing in resisting the dichotomy of gender. I still look the same; I still love dresses, make-up, and some things categorized as 'feminine.' My attachment to the performance surrounding my body and portrayal of femininity has shifted. I am Share, an agender butterfly.*

– Share Roman

A Poem for The Woman I Used To Be

Dear [dead gender]
I have not forgotten you.
Every day
Every. single. day
I think about who we would have been
if I kept you...
Bible verses, the patriarchy, and my own internalized misogyny
Who would we be today if I decided to stay in your shadow?

Never an official conversation or apology gifted to you.
No acknowledgement of your contribution to my life.

This poem is past due.
This poem is past due.

An ex-friend told me to write to you
And I couldn't before now
I *wouldn't* before now
Courage didn't live in me back then
She came as a guest but would not make a home in me.

And so,
this poem is past due.

When I first started seeing me
The lesbians around me
Chosen family
in all their magical existence
wanted to keep you in their box
I told them who I was
Explained that I was beginning to see me

"But what's wrong with being a woman and a *'she'*?"

I couldn't answer her
Thoughts ran on my tongue
but wouldn't leave my mouth
I wanted to vomit you up in front of them
I wanted to vomit you up

An ex-bae and I were sitting in his car
Eating oxtail with rice & peas
Showed him a meme – *forgot that he wasn't Queer*
He was confused with some of the language
using *'they'* as singular
After explaining that some people do not vibe with gender or boxes
The most beautiful smile, accompanied with oxtail grease
grew on the side of his mouth
"So is that what *you* are?" he asked
And for about a minute
I sat in silence, smiling too
This moment with a cishet Jamaican man
felt more affirming than ever
I felt seen, held, unjudged.

I felt you dancing inside me.
Like you were telling me, it was ok to finally let you go...

(That moment, in true cishet fashion,
was ruined by an unrelated sexist comment he made
But I digress...)

This poem is past due.

I owe you an apology.
For not checking in with you
Checking in with you,
while I was becoming *me*
And though you danced for me, I never thanked you
I never showered you with flowers
On our stage

I owe you an apology
for not acknowledging the importance you held/hold
within me
for not explaining that you
that you
were nothing to be ashamed of.

I owe you a "thank you",
for the life you've allowed me to have
to grow from
and now
for you finding comfort and safety in my memories.

I love you.

Forever grateful for you, my caterpillar.
If I blossom into a new being again,
I hope you'll still feel safe within me.

Artist Statement: *By the summer of 2016, America had endured a Trump campaign for the presidency, the PULSE nightclub shooting, the murders-caught-on-film of Alton Sterling and Philando Castile, the killing of police in Dallas and Baton Rouge, and Brock Turner was sentenced. As a mother and Native Hawaiian, the weight of all these events pressed heavily on my soul and the intersection of my own people's situation also loomed large. When the kāhea went out for writing submissions in 2022, the piece, unfortunately, was still relevant.* – Kuʻuleianuhea Awo-Chun

Color of our S(k)in

Light, dark
Darkness, light.
White, Black.
Left, right.
It's so Black and white,
Right?

Little girls watch their mothers cry.
Over their men being shot
For moving a muscle
Little boys watch their mothers cry
Over their men being shot
For being on their hustle
We all watch and cry over men being shot
For looking like trouble

How dare you move a muscle!
Pop, pop, pop.
How dare you try and hustle!
Pop, pop, pop.
Pop culture
Move, and you will get popped.

Your screen
Your school
Your friends
Your world

Says World star this
Fail army that
Says hashtag this
Trending that
Plays
Images upon images
Too graphic for television
But fine for streaming all over the Internet

Black lives matter
Blue lives matter
Brown lives matter
All lives matter
But does it matter?
How you move through this world
How you are perceived to the world
Matters
And is colored by your color
Not white and Black and blue
But
Green

And while you fight for your lives
And try your best to survive
My children cry
Our people die
Not at the hands of other men
But under the vise-like grip of chemical sin
And living on islands with no place for them

So what's a mother to do?
How do we begin
To explain to our children
The world they live in?
Are we okay knowing that
This is their inheritance?
Is this the end?
Or is it the start?

Artist Statement: *I wrote this initially at the height of burnout (and subsequently edited it for snark). The trauma inherent within the space of racial justice, scratch that, of being a mixed-race Black woman in a world that devalues me and those who look like me because of the color of an organ (which is what skin is) is magnified by social justice spaces comprised mostly of those with proximity to whiteness who are in deep denial about their own racism. Initially, it was baffling: hello, NOT immediately defaulting to denial and defensiveness is like anti-racism 101.*

Acknowledging and avoiding the very human trait of default-ing to immediate defensiveness leaves space between action and default reaction (when systemic racism is universal, be assured that a 'default reaction' to concerns of racism is rooted in white suprem-acy – don't default to that). Eventually, witnessing the status quo so deeply entrenched – even in these woke spaces – opened my eyes to the ever-present and demoralizing testament to the staying power of white supremacy in a space in which Black people should feel safe from racism, in which woke people should have some awareness of their own biases, especially in a place like Hawai'i in which there is no white majority (because it's not only white people upholding white supremacy). It is yet another space in which whiteness has taken over, harboring the same anti-Black bullshit as everywhere else.

Growing up in places where racism was NOT in short supply, it's all too familiar. It is AGAIN me balancing speaking up and being seen as "the problem" or not saying anything to prioritize white comfort at my own expense. It is AGAIN anxiety-producing straddling this line that centers whiteness (complete with the pressure to stay in my lane and perform like a good Black person is expected), while AGAIN trying to reach a group who already has made up their mind, whether about an idea, my validity as a contributor, or whatever else. I am AGAIN hyper-aware of those who have whispered to me in private, it's an issue, but in the midst of these interactions, silence is violence and is more a protest sign than an actionable response. It's AGAIN much easier for the majority to rely on tidy explanations than to deal with the real impact and insipid nature of racism from otherwise nice people. It is AGAIN avoiding fallout to protect whiteness. It is AGAIN

a textbook response in the face of racism: silence, denial, defensive-
ness...

   Acknowledging the impacts of systemic racism is incomplete
without also acknowledging how systemic racism has contributed
to the perpetuation of implicit bias. Without acknowledging implicit
bias, it can never be addressed. – Lesley G Harvey

Woke supremacy: "Good people" Racism

Those who seek change, actively pursue progress, and relentlessly
advocate for communities of care have roundly rejected the belief
that society is free from systemic racism. And for a good reason, what
lies at the end of a path of colonization, occupation, racial hierarchies,
genocide, and apathy is not a racially harmonious paradise. In Hawai'i
specifically, it is...

- 100% of HiDOE students arrested having disabilities (2017-18).[2]
- more than half of all houseless individuals identifying as Native
  Hawaiian.[3]
- Black people subject to the highest, most disproportionate, rates
  of police use of force.[4]
- a 157.9% increase of police use of force in mental health incidents.[5]

Systemic racism, that is, racism that occurs at an institutional level,
is well documented in, unsurprisingly, every major institution: from
healthcare to housing, educational access to courts and prisons, the
data is clear. Increasingly, individuals from all walks of life have taken
up the call demanding change, driven by long-term efforts or, more
recently, awakened by the unjust killing of George Floyd and countless
other BIPOCs brutalized as a consequence of racist ideals. Protests,
petitions, and public testimony confront institutional issues but do
little to counter the insidious nature of implicit bias.

2 https://s3.documentcloud.org/documents/20521930/police-in-schools-policy-brief.pdf
3 https://www.civilbeat.org/2021/01/its-time-to-acknowledge-native-hawaiians-special-
  right-to-housing/
4 https://www.civilbeat.org/2020/11/report-honolulu-police-use-of-force-increased-last-
  year/
5 https://www4.honolulu.gov/docushare/dsweb/Get/Document-288120/minutes_
  20210203.pdf (page 27)

Change requires discomfort, and, make no mistake; it is extraordinarily uncomfortable to face our own implicit biases, biases that are certainly not limited to race. This begs the question, does having implicit bias make someone a "bad" person?

Acknowledging one's own implicit bias is not a general acknowledgment that bias exists but rather a personal acknowledgment that even the *good, well-intentioned people, aka YOU, will unintentionally perpetuate bias* because *implicit bias* is not conscious and often goes against consciously held beliefs.

At the opposite end of acknowledging bias is an aversion to discomfort. It is hanging onto the belief that "doing the work" grants the do-er automatic ascension beyond individual impacts of a society that is, as evidenced by a wealth of undeniable data, systemically racist. There is no automatic exemption from perpetuating white supremacy and anti-Blackness, nor any bias for that matter. Good-intentioned people marry, give birth to, become friends with, etc., etc., people whom they *still harbor unconscious bias* because it bears repeating, *implicit bias is not conscious and often goes against consciously held beliefs.*

Be honest with yourself; what feelings arise when you say aloud, '*I am not exempt from implicit bias and from perpetuating anti-Blackness and white supremacy*'? Discomfort? Disbelief? Denial? Let that go. Implicit bias is imposed upon all of us from birth. It is the images, and themes repeated day in and day-out throughout our entire existence that impact.us. Without exception. Think of it like the existence of gravity: it's there, weighing us down every day, whether acknowledged or not makes no difference: it exists.

Aversion to discomfort, otherwise known as the right to comfort, can perhaps be seen more clearly in conservative extremists' intentional efforts to lie about racism's prominent place in U.S. history. It is a never-ending news cycle reminding us that conservative comfort, in which a person may experience feelings of discomfort in learning about racism (in other words, empathy, you know exactly what humans should feel when learning about murder, brutality, oppression, and violence) is weighted more heavily than the discomfort of *experiencing racism – experiencing murder, brutality, oppression, and violence – felt by the victims of racism.* No.

For activists, advocates, and allies, or those in, shall we say, woke spaces, there is a concerted and no-doubt, well-intentioned focus on external efforts to address institutional racism. That's all well and good and absolutely a part of the equation (racist policies exist, intentional or otherwise). The problem is when these external efforts are *at the exclusion* of acknowledging individual implicit racial bias, perpetuated regardless of conscious belief.

Everyday vernacular peppered with buzzwords like *inclusive* and *ally* is of little comfort on the path to progress when that path is corroded by the same denial racism that exists in the current system(ically racist systems). When "the work" is nothing more than a performance, those moments of discomfort that would otherwise reveal areas requiring deep, personal *unlearning or reevaluating or tuning into* are fraught with textbook white fragility violence: denial, defensiveness, disregard, dismissal, and silence. Add a heaping dose of *woke* tone-policing, topped with entitlement to comfort, and we're left with "racial justice activists who carry privilege and entitlement into racial justice movements" (Gorski, 2019), keeping "good people" firmly rooted in white supremacist delusion. In other words, more racism.

Denial (as well as defensiveness, disregard, dismissal, and silence in the face) of racism *is racism*. Acknowledging that EVERYONE, *without exception*, perpetuates implicit bias is a requirement on the path to addressing and rooting out racism. In the same manner, it's important to acknowledge the racist history of this country (errr, world – *global colonizing, I'm looking at you*) in classroom discourse (AND IN EVERYTHING because...it affects EV.ERY.THING), it is an absolute imperative for those in *woke spaces* to also turn that attention inwards. Sure, this kind of radical self-awareness is likely to produce feelings of discomfort. Fortunately, we're all in the same ~~boat~~ storm; there is no change nor progress without discomfort. For all of us. There is no exception to that rule. Are non-Black allies ready to face the discomfort?

In a word, no. Performing *"not racist"* is one thing. It requires time out of the day but few surprises and minimal *personal discomfort or sacrifice* (outside of time). It's mostly comfortable because the performance ends, the "not racist" sash comes off, and the clever slogans and cutesy signs can be put away until the next *performance.*

It is in the unexpected moments, particularly in woke spaces as evidenced, that reveal whether an individual is willing to face *personal discomfort and sacrifice* to acknowledge that "good intentions" and "good people," aka YOU, are not exempt from perpetuating white supremacy. The composition of social justice spaces overwhelmingly reflects historically powerful and historically privileged systems — a visible manifestation, rooted in unacknowledged white supremacy, of the disconnect between conceptual ideology and reality. Coupled with all those "good intentions" and the echo chamber of those who are historically well-represented, it culminates into an added layer of *not racist* ego identity that's ripe for denial.

Transformation won't happen in spaces built on white supremacy, no matter how well-intentioned, no matter how many woke "good people" comprise the space, and no matter how many protest signs with clever slogans. Building from a foundation of unacknowledged white supremacy and anti-Blackness replicates the same systems, with a dose of woke.

Perpetuating white supremacy is pervasive and insidious, not limited to a Black/White issue, especially not in Hawaiʻi. Hawaiʻi's historically powerful and -privileged are overwhelmingly East Asian, White (passing), and, same as everywhere, affluent. Being non-White doesn't exempt a person from perpetuating white supremacy. Having Black friends or engaging in activist pursuits doesn't make a person any less anti-Black than having daughters or a mom makes someone less misogynistic. Denial perpetuates the systemic structures of harm. In all cases.

Cultivating transformation is about total change. Change comes with discomfort. It's going against the status quo by speaking out, *even when it is uncomfortable.* There is no surer sign of "I am not safe" than immediate denial of any racism – frankly, it's in the same vein as someone attempting to convince others that gravity doesn't impact them: totally delusional. You are not that special. I am not that special. We are not exempt from reality and truth simply because we are so exceptional.

Giving up privilege and divesting from whiteness – by now, I hope it's apparent that *whiteness* is not about skin color but about perpetuating a racial hierarchy that centers whiteness – is about a willingness to *personally sacrifice* to make the world more equitable. It's not comfortable. It's not an "everyone else" issue. We all have to be willing to accept there are things about ourselves that will need to change; that we can perpetuate harm even when we don't mean to; that intentions do not outweigh impact; that the default centers white comfort; and that while our current conditions are limiting, new perspectives and challenges to our belief are transformative. There is no growth without *personal* discomfort. Continuing to center the feelings and comfort of the historically-privileged and -powerful comes *at the cost of change.* The key to weathering all that discomfort is reframing discomfort as a sign of growth to look back and then decide now, *I won't be the same person I was yesterday because I do not want the world to be the same as it was yesterday.*

None of the above is limited to race. We all harbor various biases. That's a problem, but it's not *the problem.* The problem is a refusal to acknowledge it. When we can acknowledge the issue (whether individual bias or systemic racism), we can address it. It is the only way to forge a new path and sow the seeds of transformation.

A Static Dynamic

Deysha Childs

Moving and free?
I'm moving in solace.
Yet, I'm seen.
Heard? Maybe.
Glass ceilings.
I see opaque people prancing.
But they're walking in place.
How is that a way to win a race?
How is that a way to win a race?
Even allied is a forbidden attitude.
Static entropy,
Chaotic heat.
Why won't you move?
Too explosive.
Watching static electricity
tingle at my being.
Like the lamps, I used to touch.
So amazed I never felt
lightning like us, dynamic see.
See.
Do you really
want true love on Earth to be?
Or is this Jack and Rose?
Romeo and Juliet?
Two forces of duality
never meant to have met.
Dynamic stress.

Artist Statement: *This poem is about resisting false binaries of hope and progress when used as a balm or excuse to not expect more of ourselves and our society.* – Jess Heard

Dystopia

Dystopia is a fine mist

So gray and hazy
you'd swear it was raining

But no one can see it

In the thick fog called progress
you're told to be patient
and feel grateful it's not pouring
And if you'd only look more closely
there's clearly hope around the bend

You're made to feel silly
for using your umbrella

Though no one seems to notice
everyone is drenched
In denial

Artist Statement: *For my submission, I theorize through my embodied youth experiences having grown up in urban Kalihi with other racialized and working-class Oceanic youth in the 1990s/2000s. I recount the ways my relationships with other Oceanic youth from different militarized/colonial histories and state-based relationships to the U.S. came together and built cultural identities grounded in Kalihi and other forms of youth subcultures to evade, move through, and resist everyday oppression. It is through this lens that I attempt to break down Native/Settler, immigrant/Local, gay/straight, whore/virgin, light/dark, good/bad binaries to foreground how community and cultures of resistance are being made on the ground. Drawing inspiration from and thinking alongside the brilliance of Black writers and activists, I conclude with how the rebellious culture of my youth has led me to identify and align myself with all rebellious movements for Black, Brown, and Indigenous decolonial and abolitionist justice in Hawai'i and beyond in my adulthood.* – Demiliza Sagaral Saramosing

A Filipina Hood Feminist Perspective: Youth Culture and The Politics of Feeling Good in Working-Class Kalihi

Girls in the hood have to navigate stressors, bury traumas, and still carve out the space to be human... The hood is still home, but they have to look beyond the troubled streets they are on every day and see themselves as worth saving.
–Mikki Kendall, "Hood Feminism: Notes from the Woman That a Movement Forgot."

Pleasure activism is the work we do to reclaim our whole, happy, and satisfiable selves from the impacts, delusions, and limitations of oppression and/or supremacy.
–adrienne maree brown, "Pleasure Activism: The Politics of Feeling Good."

Growing up in Kalihi, I loved *feeling good.* When I say, "good," I don't mean "proper." Though, I do admit that there was this fleeting and entertaining joy I felt when I role-played the "good" Filipina in Hawai'i.

I mastered code-switching in middle school when I saw how "playing good" got me respect and praise from administrators, teachers, and on-campus security in our messed-up education system. It gave me a sense of power and control in an environment that often disrespected and downplayed my authority as a girl of color. Growing up in the 90s/2000s, "playing good" allowed me to level up, to gain clout, and to evade punishment. I "played good" to navigate an education system that cared more about students tucking in our shirts, wearing mid-knee skirts, speaking "straight" English, and winning scholarly awards, proving to other schools that, in fact, "good" youth citizens and soon-to-be successful workers can indeed emerge from this island ghetto. In Kalihi, I learned from a young age that the landscape of this game called life was a confusing one. Trying to understand my place in the world growing up as a young Filipina meant trying to decipher my identity entrenched in mixed messages: "don't learn how to speak Filipino and be FOB / don't talk pidgin or you'll sound stupid," "we go beach / don't get dark," "be skinny and sexy / don't spread your legs and be one slut / don't act like a boy." In order for me to gain favor and rise above the odds stacked against me, I studied closely the ins and outs on what it meant to win at survival in Kalihi. I became keenly aware of the opportune moments to strategically "play good" to reap the benefits from a system that I knew was not for me. "Playing good" meant knowing the right moments to smile more, speak in a soft and sweet voice, keep my head down, myself out of trouble and away from the sun, and dress more feminine and conservative so as to not send "the wrong message."

I do wonder if I had "played good," because I was also afraid of being treated badly like my friends who never held back their voices and fists against the respectable middle- to upper-class expectations of higher-ups. I am learning to heal my PTSD rooted in surviving my girlhood experiences now that I am in adulthood. I realize that respectability politics, or as defined by the Black author and hood feminist Mikki Kendall, the "attempt by marginalized groups to internally police members so that they fall in line with the dominant culture's norms," in this settler colonial system does not save any of us. Gaining acceptance from carceral and settler state institutions that have pressured me to "play good" was and continues to be damaging to my body, mind, and spirit. For this reason, I firmly believe that we must refuse it. Now, I want to turn my attention from "playing good" to actually *feeling good*. I understand "playing good" as a performance I used to navigate and survive the over-policing of my youth experiences at home, school, church, the streets of Kalihi. Drawing inspiration from the queer Black feminist writer adrienne maree brown, I understand her concept of *feeling good* as an embodied experience. Accessing the means to *feel good* in my body allowed me to escape the pressures of everyday life. *Feeling good* meant getting lost in pleasure to be my most realist and defiant self. I trace my genealogy to the long tradition of Indigenous and Women of Color feminist praxis discussed in the landmark anthology, "This Bridge Called My Back: Writings by Radical Women of Color," co-edited by Cherríe Moraga and Gloria Anzaldúa. I borrow Cherríe Moraga's concept of theory in the flesh: *Stay with me as I curate and offer my body as an archive and portal to seeing abundant pleasures in Kalihi.*

For my sisters Sara Lee, Sherina, and I, the urban neighborhood of Kalihi was our backyard that we shared with all the other neighborhood kids. When we were old enough to be given our own keys to let ourselves in our family's two-bedroom apartment while our parents were working long hours, we would quickly run home from school, drop our bags on the floor, and run back outside to cruise it with our friends. We were exhausted from school. We were tired of having to prove that we were more than just some "dumb Kalihi kids," a phrase we often heard growing up in our 96817/96819 zip codes. This is why us grungy mixed group of kids, sometimes 15 or 20 of us, often from Ilokano, Bisayan, Tagalog, Vietnamese, Kānaka Maoli, Chuukese, Marshallese, Tongan, and Sāmoan ancestries would often congregate to places like our apartment complex's "Merry-Go-Round" (courtyard) to drift into our own dreamscape of (pop) punk rock, kawaii, and skate cultures. Together, some of us read manga, and some of us bloodied our knees skateboarding while ollie-ing off and eating it at Kalihi-Kai elementary school's out-door stage. Some of us also busted out laughing while recording the whole fiasco on our flip phones. Our lively and most heated debates revolved around fashion. For example, is that person's style more emo, punk, or scene?

Like so many other girls, I was into style-crossings between Japanese anime girl characters and Paramore band's lead vocalist Hayley Williams. I sported straightened, thinned-out blonde/brown highlighted hair with side swept bangs, fake thick-rimmed Hello Kitty glasses, thrift shop graphic tees, and Black shorts from Hot Topic and Savers, striped knee-high socks, fishnets, brightly colored sex bracelets, studded belts, and classic Black converse high-tops. My friends and I spent long hours listening to our burned CDs on our SONY walkmans, head-banged to, and loudly sang along to the songs from our favorite bands despite our neighbors telling us to shut up and move: Paramore, The Pettit Project, All American Rejects, Taking Back Sunday, Green Day, Blink 182, My Chemical Romance, Yellowcard, The Summer Obsession, and so many more. We jammed out to their rebellious messages while throwing fireworks at and inside abandoned Foodland Shopping carts, watching them melt and burst into tall orange flames. We were high on feeling good listening to these bands. We really felt like they wrote these songs for us brown Kalihi kids, take for instance, us listening to the song The Great Escape by Boys Like Girls while running down Dillingham Boulevard: *Throw it away/Forget yesterday/We'll make the great escape/ we won't hear a word they say/They don't know us anyway/Watch it burn/Let it die/'Cause we are finally free tonight!*

I was excellent at "playing good" when I started going to Farrington High School. I roamed freely through the halls because I was perceived as running off to do "smart girl" kine things like taking leadership roles in the Student Council. But what the teachers and security didn't know was that I sometimes skipped class to go to my ex-boyfriend's house to make-out. I savored white gummy bear-flavored Jamba Juice on my tongue post-makeout sessions. I would daydream in class and repeatedly write on my marble notebook pages: *Oh my gosh, I love him (and him, aNd HiM, and HIM sOo MuCh)!* I was addicted to the feeling of falling in love, being able to slow-dance at Peter Buck Park, and clinging onto someone, who I once claimed, used to be my world. One of my exes stole brand-named shirts from Alaz and Pearlz for me, which I proudly wore, even when removing the security sensors left holes in them. Another one got his ass beat by

my guy friends for calling me a slut at school—that brought me justice.
I enjoyed the thrill of playing spin-the-bottle and truth-or-dare with
all my friends, knowing that choosing "dare" was so much more fun.
Hanging out with girlfriends at Kamz brought me joy. We stole Black
liquid eyeliner from Longs Drugs and took turns painting thin streaks
onto one another's eyelids. We tried on dresses at Jeans Warehouse
in search of our outfits to the winter formal dances, modeled them
in front of the dressing room mirrors, and confided in one another
on which dresses made our boobs look good. Everywhere we went
was our dance floor– from our cramped bedrooms, we shared with
other family members, in front of Kalihi-Palama Library where the
cold-water fountains stay, to the extravagant hotel ballrooms of
Waikīkī. We used Windows Movie Maker to create our lip-sync and
dancing videos that we posted onto YouTube, where we embodied
divas such as Destiny's Child power-trio: *I'm a survivor/I'm gonna
make it/I will survive/Keep on survivin'!* At our school dances, we
kicked off our heels, swayed our hips, flipped our hair, and in unruly
rows, we freak-danced against one another to the bumpin' beats of
Usher, *'cause baby, tonight/the DJ got us falling in love again!* and the
rhythm of Rihanna, *Please don't stop the music! Mama-say, mama-sa,
ma-ma-ko-ssa!*

After graduating from high school, I worked at Blazin' Steaks Kalihi
while attending the University of Hawai'i at Mānoa. Blazin' Steaks was
poppin' because it was so cheap: $6.50 steak plate with two scoops of
rice, macaroni salad on the side, and a free drink. In between rush-
hours, my co-workers and I wiped table-tops and cleaned restrooms
while skanking to songs from our favorite reggae bands such as Iration,
Kolohe Kai, Rebel Souljahz, and Ekolu. We "accidentally" over-packed
our "one free meal" plates after work that we later took home to our
families. Since I was stationed at the front register, I flirted with the
military guys who came through – *oh hey, how are you? ;)* *singsong
voice* The big tips they left behind often funded my weekend shenan-
igans. My sisters and I were party promoters–#TheSaramosingSisters
seen throughout the early days of social media platforms MySpace,
Facebook, and Instagram. I was always the DJ's +1 guest. PLURR was
life, and carpooling around town with my friends selling tickets for

Honolulu's party scene felt like an urgent mission we had to accomplish. When the night came, the magic began. $20/pop. Wait for the bass to drop. Hardstyle. House dance. Minty fresh Vicks Vapor mist. Teary eyes. Hot multi-colored flashing lights illuminated bodies in the dark. Leaning back against electrifying loudspeakers. Warm breath against sweaty necks. Cool island breeze. Intoxicating cuddle puddles, peaking hard, feeling security in a stranger's arms. We wished those moments would last forever. Bailey's vocals took us into the clouds: *Somehow you wipe my tears away/Forever I hold you close to me/In the fields of summer here I lay/I'm caught in a trance/a higher state.*

As kids growing up in Kalihi, the fact that we were part of the "working-class" in this racial capitalist and occupying settler state of Hawai'i engaged in the ongoing struggles against imperialism, militarism, and colonialism never crossed our minds. For most of us, the everyday battles that were important to us and the tactics we deployed against our everyday oppressions fell outside the walls of what most people think of as traditional or mainstream youth activism, working-class labor struggles, and decolonial politics. I've never known anyone back in the day to talk about our place in "decolonial" and "demilitarization" movements in Hawai'i. For the most part, mainstream activist spaces can be inaccessible and alienating to the working-class. Rather, I've known those who repped Kalihi HARD through cultural venues, rituals, and practices such as music, making stink-eye at those looking down on Kalihi, dancing, scrapping, graffiti of private property, unapologetic T-Shirts with "Kalihi: The City with No Pity," emblazoned across their chests, and "cheeee-hooooooos" for those doing big things coming out of Kalihi, making Kalihi proud. This is what I am most interested in. I understand these defiant cultural hybrid energies coming up from the ash, grit, and concrete rubble of Kalihi as an important site of resistance from the violence of poverty, policing, and cultural assimilation. I write this as I am inspired by and thinking relationally with the Black historian Robin D. G. Kelley's book *Race Rebels*, that centers the daily lives of Black working-class people, pleasures, and politics that have been relegated to the margins of Black politics and labor activism. Borrowing Kelley's ideas to aid me in understanding my youth experiences in Hawai'i's peculiar, racialized socio-economic and political context, I believe that we Kalihi kids fought for justice against everyday oppression on the terrains that was oftentimes, "cultural, centering on identity, dignity, and fun." We built new cultures, strategies of resistance, identities, sexualities, etc., in response to oppression. We turned our bodies into instruments of fun and pleasure every chance we got.

Oftentimes, the mainstream "heroic" forms of activism that are led by middle-class representatives overshadow these day-to-day resistances of "ordinary" working-class people. Instead of dismissing my working-class youth experiences as manifestations of immaturity, false consciousness, or primitive rebellion, I want you, dear reader, to dig beneath the surface of political institutions and organized social movements. Immerse yourselves into the daily lives, cultures, and communities which make the working classes so much more than people who labor or who are exploited workers pipelined into our military and tourism economy. I am not discrediting mainstream decolonial and demilitarization movements. In fact, I am trying to suggest ways to connect the struggles and cultural resistances of "ordinary" working-class people just trying to survive on a day-to-day basis to our mainstream formal politics. Although the cultural rebellions of my own youth experiences in Kalihi might not seem like extraordinary events and are marginal to the "main organizing efforts," they held powerful significance for me in debunking the notion of Hawai'i as a multi-racial paradise. I am a Filipina who carries the cultural resistance strategies and knowledges of my ancestors as well as my youth experiences in my body. These gritty embodied knowledges have allowed me to access empowerment opportunities and navigate the tumultuous terrains of higher education. All throughout my 20s, I have learned from mentors in academia and grassroots community organizing spaces new languages and tools to name and challenge violent power structures. This led me to identify and politically align myself with all rebellious movements – both taking place within and outside of established organizations and institutions – for Black, Brown, and Indigenous justice in Hawai'i and beyond in my adulthood. I share my embodied working-class youth experiences in Kalihi to show the radical potential of harnessing, nurturing, and invoking cultural politics and pleasurable experiences for subversive and coalitional means. It is through centering the cultural politics of *feeling good* from this "way, way below" approach that I believe we can re-fuel, re-energize, and reimagine new ways to grow our ongoing decolonization and abolitionist movements grounded in ea (life, land, and sovereignty) in Hawai'i.

Disclaimer: The events depicted in this narrative nonfiction are told as I, the author, remembers them. Names are not included, characters are combined, and events are compressed.

Black of the Earth in the Black of My Birth

Ahmad Selim Aboagye Xallen

Asase Yaa in my mother
My mother in me
Asase Yaa in my birth
Thursday
Yaw
What was the name of my grandmother's tree?

Black of the earth
Black of my birth
A time of comfort
A time of mirth
A time of shame
A time of pain

We have both been exhumed
Violently
Torn out of crying mothers
Snatched and processed
Expectations already in mind
Nothing positive
Nothing kind
Denigrated
Like filth
Like mud
Like dirt
Never like soil

Sacred
Life giving
Nurturing nourishing
Pure
Not in the sense of sterile whiteness
But in a sense of rich, life-giving Blackness

Pure
In the sense that she is the original and unaltered, the one
   and the unfalter
-ing,

lush has lost its ability to attach
purity with a sense of comfort and unity
Soil with richness, richness and wealth with earth,
earth to nurturing, nurturing to mother

WITHOUT obligations to anyone else besides her children

But we have forgotten to attach the word
mother to the idea of someone
EVERYONE has some kind of obligation to
The one(s) who raised, nourished, and cared for you

We have forgotten to attach the word Black to the smell of fertile soil
The dream of full gardens, full bellies, and full hearts
Full oceans full of fish
Full skies full of stars
Full galaxies
Full lives

My soul

Ahmad Selim Aboagye Xallen

My soul does not yet have a name
I don't not know what to call it nor what name it answers to
But I can definitely tell you how it feels

First of all it feels like me
With all the pretty and all the ugly
Weighty and weighted and waiting
Not like a weight
More like something else heavy
Something comforting

Heavy like a home
With enough walls to hold my heart
To offer rest to loved ones
And strangers
Who could one day be loved ones
Or not

More like something else heavy
Something fruitful
Like a tree loaded with fruits
But also loaded with flowers
Floral scents mixing with bee buzzing
mixed with round little spheres
waiting to be shared
Heavy with potential and growth
and age and stories and wisdom
All at the same time

More like something else heavy
Something vast
Like a roaring ocean in a roaring storm
At night
No up or down or in or out
Just presence
And volatility
When's the last time you smelled the sea in a storm?

My soul also dances, but that's a given.
We're all souls dancing to our own beat in unison.

Community Impact Design Projects

Our 2020-2021 Youth Series focused on the exploration, analysis, and evolution of our ancestral, individual, and collective stories of resistance and liberation. Our culminating project included the creation of a Community Impact Design project. This project incorporated the Pillars of Liberation and our Meta-Themes of Resistance. The four meta-themes of resistance are: countering cultural hegemony; accountability; resistance to false binaries; and reconstruction of cultural memory. The meta themes and their significance to our community impact goals were articulated in Billye Raushanah Smith's thesis: Countering Hegemony Through Synthesis: A Lifetime Of Commitment To The Black Community In The Works Of Toni Cade Bambara. The Pillars of Liberation were identified by Pūlama Long and are the: Institutions/Structures/people/community organizations; Ideologies/Methodology/Education; and Values/Behaviors/Beliefs that support our vision for change.

Our learning model was deeply inspired by the Story Project Model, developed by LeeAnne Bell. The Storytelling Project Model categorizes and describes four types of stories: (1) stock stories, (2) concealed stories, (3) resistance stories, and (4) emerging/transforming stories. We began by challenging stock stories in Hawai'i's marginalized communities while unearthing concealed stories that are just beneath the surface and challenging the dominant white narrative that distorts Black/Brown/Indigenous stories (Bell).

As we unearthed the concealed stories from our cultural and ancestral memory, and research (we gathered stories from books, articles, essays, community surveys, and our interactions with the community), we were able to locate our stories of resistance. From our stories of resistance, we identified four meta-themes: cultural memory, accountability, resisting false binaries, and countering hegemony. These four themes of resistance became the foundation of the participants' Community Impact Design projects.

An online digital diary allowed participants to share and reflect on their experiences, reflections, and evolution in the program, as well as any creative writing they wished to share with the group. The online diary was inspired by the work of Binahkaye Joy, founder of the Fertility Abundance Garden, "a sanctuary for mothers, a congregation for creators, a dreamscape for sacred storytellers."

Our space was initiated and maintained by our relationship with the stories of our ancestors, the land that nourishes us, and our spiritual well-being. Nana Sula, the Youth's resident ancestral guide and Elder, facilitated this space's integrity. We offered individual check-in sessions with interested participants in between workshop and mentorship sessions. The purpose of these sessions was to strengthen our relationships with each participant since a large zoom call does not allow for intimate communication. Moreover, it allowed us to support a deeper engagement with the themes explored during our workshop sessions. Our year together was a turbulent one as we were all navigating the pandemic and long-standing injustices and inequities that amplified its impact on our communities. Having a space to unpack our experiences and feelings during this year was an invaluable gift for all of us in the program.

Youth participants generated questions from the stories and themes we explored in our workshops. These questions served to help participants better understand the program's content and our own stories as they were evolving. Further, the responses from our online community helped to inform the youth's Community Impact Design projects as we required that the intervention reflected the lived experiences of our community rather than the stock stories and assumptions which so often inform our response to community challenges. The survey questions our youth asked of our community included questions like: How did you survive this past summer? What kind of physical or mental space do you go to for healing? In your community, what healing spaces are lacking? What resources do you have available? What is your vision of healing? What steps do we take to decolonize the student body? Is it in our language that we review our own studies?

Members from our Hawai'i community and abroad who had experience in resistance and liberation work were invited to share their stories during our workshops and during one-on-one mentorship sessions. Guest speakers and mentors represented a range of issues, stories, and communities. Participants were provided with books covering a range of issues and communities. All books were provided with the support of our community. For more information on our guest speakers and mentors, please see the bio section at the start of this book.

Ahmad Selim Aboagye Xallen

COMMUNITY IMPACT DESIGN PROJECT

Hibiscus Hour

Hibiscus Hour is an open discussion space in which traditional Healers, plant specialists, environmental specialists, cultural practitioners, healthcare workers, and an interested audience can come together and discuss relationships with plants, people, environment, and health as well as the many different places in which these groups intersect. Unlike many other healing spaces, this one is also open to those who have been wholesale disconnected from their indigeneity, spirituality, and humanity. A short-term goal is to put practitioners from different cultural backgrounds into meaningful and non-abrasive conversations with each other.

The initial goal is to expand circles of relationships and deepen relationships between practitioners, practices, and people. Eventually, I would like the Hibiscus Hour to expand into workshops, workdays, and policy change. Some of the most important outcomes this project can work towards is giving marginalized oceanic voices another platform to communicate on. Hopefully, this project can help to foster meaningful relationships in which communities hold one another accountable. NO STEALING OF MEDICINE. Hopefully, this event can help to cultivate values of community empowerment, concern for one another, and curiosity about community health and healing. It should also expand ideas of community. This workshop should open up opportunities for deepening relationships and trust between traditional health systems and "western" health systems. Participants should be able to build different frameworks of guiding questions, stories, and experiences, as well as tap into their community networks in order to explore what works best for them.

The workshop itself was envisioned to be in a comfortable, casual, community gathering place in which people could share food and stories. Ideally, our different community healers would sit together in a small circle or semicircle in which they could face each other. The normal single-file seating of a panel complicates the panelists' ability to interact with one another. This setting formation includes the moderator/host and encourages direct discussion. Various topics could range from something like "what use does okra have in your culture?" to "the 5 senses: What does a healthy community look, smell, feel, taste, and sound like?"

However, due to COVID-19, I did not feel comfortable hosting an in-person meeting. I also was not able to get in contact with enough community "professionals" to have them discuss with one another and have the general community listen. As an alternative, I will offer the workshop online.

Hibiscus Hour Guiding Discussion Questions:
1. What do you think of when you see these plants?
2. When you think of these plants, what places come to mind for you?
3. What stories do you have with these plants?
4. What uses do you or your family have for these plants?
5. What are your relations to these plants?
6. What kinds of relationships would you like to build and grow?

Aurora Jeffrey

COMMUNITY IMPACT DESIGN PROJECT

Six Guideposts for a Decolonial Classroom Philosophy

If we're talking destinies and what we are here for, my body, heart, and mind has always aspired to illuminate the truth and light others carry. From Mrs. Menezes' first-grade class on, I was determined to channel my energy into my own loving, foundational first-grade classroom. 20 years later, I am not sure classroom teaching is specifically the work my ancestors empowered me to do. In the meantime, the "Weaving Our Stories" community gave me an outlet to abolish my own respectability standards, develop my personal education philosophy utilizing the four pillars of resistance, and incorporate it all into a curriculum for early childhood education.

It was only in college when teachers gave me permission to critique the rules that I began to understand the imperfections of "respectability" and its function as social control. Then, it was only after entering a classroom recently to teach that I noticed the prevalence of respectability in a five- or six-year-old's eyes. You're not supposed to talk about poop or farting. You're not supposed to walk barefoot. These practices are rooted in imperialism, white supremacy, and contemporary gendered violence.

Colonization estranges people from land and from our bodies. Our bodies are used as justification for our oppression. The product is that our bodies and the land are where we see the impact of injustice. Estranging ourselves from our own bodies' natural processes and function conditions us to a practice of dissection. We dissect our bodies into what is considered human, "civilized", "respectable." We identify human emotion or behavior as primitive and inferior. Decolonial pedagogy has to reintegrate us to the land we live with and the bodies that carry us through life.

My project questions how we decolonize the classroom. First, I considered the four pillars of resistance to help attune myself to a decolonial pedagogy. With that framework, I created 6 guideposts of my suggested teaching philosophy to reflect these pillars in a class-room setting.

Four pillars of resistance

accountability | resisting false binaries
reconstructing cultural memory | countering cultural hegemony

Six guideposts of my suggested teaching philosophy
1. Abolish Respectability
2. Encourage Success Through Collaboration
3. Body-Based Anti-oppression Framework
4. Social Emotional Learning
5. Cite Your Sources
6. Sustainability (nature & emotions)

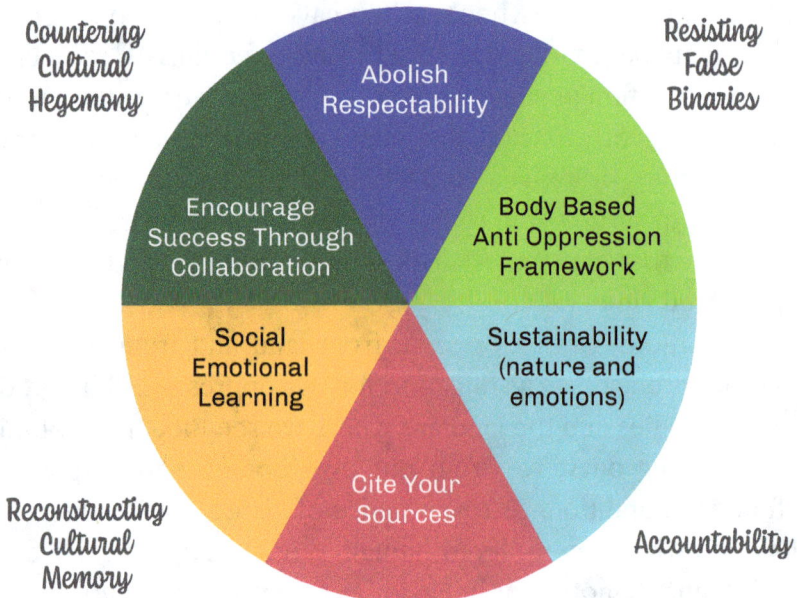

Countering Cultural Hegemony

Resisting False Binaries

Abolish Respectability

Body Based Anti Oppression Framework

Encourage Success Through Collaboration

Social Emotional Learning

Sustainability (nature and emotions)

Cite Your Sources

Reconstructing Cultural Memory

Accountability

Abolish respectability

Rules that govern respectability hold judgmental reasoning. To avoid policing movement and speech in the name of "respectability," behavioral expectations should correspond to classroom values. By teaching children to abide by rules that have no basis, we teach them not to critique. And we are often teaching them to be ashamed of their natural bodies. Students, no matter their age, deserve a good reason for any rules, temporary or permanent, that exist.

Goals should correspond to a classroom value. Expectations of any kind, be it academic evaluation or the proper form when sitting at your desk, need to be grounded in virtue. Don't allow perception or external validation to be a justification for anything in your classroom.

Encourage success through collaboration

I worry that individualized grades focus on the value of one over the collective. This can cause anxiety in learning spaces which should be playful and innovative. The hope with this guidepost is to encourage teachers to move from a culture of comparative evaluation to one of collaboration. If we emphasize collaboration as the metric of success, could we also enhance the main purpose of education: learning? Additionally, if we reframe success through collaboration, we can view the teacher as a part of the classroom system not above or behind it.

Body-based anti-oppression framework

This idea is multipronged, but its main function is reconstructing cultural memory. As psychology catches up to the millions-of-years project that is the human brain, we are learning that DNA in our bodies changes in response to trauma that our parents and grandparents experienced. This fascinating field is known as epigenetics. There is also easily recognized stress that ensues when people confront hegemonic structures. Our heart rate increases, we sweat, and we tense. For that reason, we need education to incorporate activities that awaken our awareness of our bodies. It is the teaching of breathing, regulation, and advocacy for what is right for each person's body.

Social emotional learning

What if we gave young children a vocabulary of injustice? Teach them to analyze privilege, which is to recognize power; teach them to notice their wants and needs so they can be aware of when someone is not acting in their best interest. I imagine a new kind of civic program in schools. More of a curriculum for consent that provides students, from a young age, with an interpersonal tool kit to manage their relationships healthily, whether friendship, familial, or, eventually, professional.

We live in a world of competition and manipulating ourselves to function against our mental and physical needs. By positioning this curriculum from a framework of historical oppression, we immediately address the tension of the lessons with the students' realities. As they grow in the world, they are taught to notice the contradictions of social myths such as meritocracy, wealth, and individualism instead of being asked to contort themselves within it.

Cite your sources

To a certain extent, teachers are gatekeepers of knowledge. When there is knowledge passed between people, it is a big responsibility. Teachers hold more power in this exchange and, therefore, should be held accountable for the information they share. To avoid the truth being fully co-opted by misinformation, these gatekeepers of knowledge should reference primary sources as often as possible and be wary of where their information is coming from.

Sustainability (nature and emotions)

Just as we have only one Earth, we also have only one body. Incorporating ideas of sustainable living requires one to be in tune with the relationship between the mind-body and the environment. In the classroom, this means remaining in a space where challenges help you learn, not exhaust you. Additionally, it means putting our theories of justice into practice for all living things. Teaching should be the act of all the best ideas and learnings. Classrooms are systems within a school system. The structure of the school system should function to support the needs of the classroom system, bottom up.

Breena Thompson

COMMUNITY IMPACT DESIGN PROJECT
Healing through Scrapbooking

I had to recently write a paper for my ethnic studies class on any topic that I saw fit. I chose to talk about the Black folk on campus. I wanted to talk about our lack of safe spaces and everything we endure in these learning spaces. I have felt alone on campus and so have others. We need somewhere to process our isolation, but when it comes to therapy and finding a Black therapist, you have to know where to go or be in a certain area. It seems like Black students can only find safety and community on certain campuses, but we should not feel alone almost everywhere we go. Every Black student I interviewed had an experience with racism, and all felt so alone here. Hawai'i is portrayed in the media as having no racism, but that's not true. Black students can't escape what we go through and, yet, are yet told to get over it and ignore it. It's not healthy to ignore it and, besides. we can't. Even in places of learning, there are laws that prevent us from talking about race, yet the trauma and disrespect, and discrimination is something we have to live with forever.

Did you know that the part of the population that identifies as Black or African American has reported having over 16% with mental health issues? This is over 7 million people. Black and African Americans are less likely to die from suicide but are more likely to attempt suicide (9.8% v 6.1%.) The rise in thoughts, plans, and attempts of suicide is on the rise. Back in 2008 the total was 443,000 for combined; as of 2018 it is at 716,000.[6]

My goal for my Community Impact Design project is to provide a safe space for Black and African American youth and adults to be able to speak out on issues they are experiencing. Through scrapbooking and discussion, we will address these issues in a safe space.

The impact I want this to have on the community is for participants to feel that they are in a safe space, where they feel like we are family. I want us to relax and see how important talking, drawing, and writing is in helping relieve stress as we address our mental health. I am hoping this will work because there is such a lack of opportunities for the community to get proper help or to even have a proper space that they can feel comfortable enough in to share.

Addressing our themes of resistance

I feel as though our cultural memory is rooted in pain and silence. We are known as "strong" people, so we never get the chance to think about our feelings in a healthy way. I want to change that by offering space for healing in a way that can be looked back on as a part of our collective cultural memory.

We are countering cultural hegemony by going against the association that just one culture or group of people have mental health issues. I've only ever seen one group of people focused on when mental health is discussed, and I think it's time to change that. The Black community and the white community have different access to

6 https://www.mhanational.org/issues/Black-and-african-american-communities-and-mental-health

mental health care because of false binaries. We all need help, and we need to talk about mental health.

We hold accountability within ourselves and ask that of our community. We start by holding accountable the first person that tells us to stop crying or belittles our feelings and mental health. That could be a parent or a grandparent or even ourselves. We can speak up for ourselves and others.

Deysha Childs

COMMUNITY IMPACT DESIGN PROJECT

Healing through Planting

Drugs and mental health, in my opinion, go hand in hand. I think that cultivating a sense of community is important. A sense of community and people nearby that care about others well being, can help aid depression, anxiety, anger, and other mental health issues.

Depleted mental health often leads to escapism. Oftentimes, our unexpressed emotions find a way of expressing themselves in destructive ways. Ultimately, I think that pharmaceuticals are for the greater good when addressing mental health issues. However, bringing cultural memory to native holistic approaches when aiding mental health can drastically not only combat cultural hegemony, and resist false binaries, it may also bring about accountability.

My entire time living in Honolulu, I've been familiar with the substance abuse that goes on in the area. I have always considered

This is Lo'i Kalo. Historically this mini park located in Kalihi was was apart of the Kapalama taro agricultural intelligence system of Natives. I was inclined to take these photos to represent not only the beauty of this historical park, but also the restorative ideas I've thought of living three minutes away. There are plenty non native plants inhabiting this site. The water has also been tainted and no longer really irrigates. The stock story in my opinion is, "here lies a hidden Kalihi gem." Which is true. However, it is also concealed alongside trafficking and alcoholism. It used to be a site for healing and restoratively I imagine that for the people who hang out here; but to create healthier coping mechanisms and an opportunity to teach and show healthy support within the community. Accountability is what I see shown in these images, we see noble people are cleaning up the area and making it beautiful. My accountability is also I was too shy to ask if I could help. Likewise, the taro patches reveal the reconstruction of cultural memory. All in all, I imagine this park being a place for gardening, planting native plants and healing. A place people can talk story and get their hands dirty to remember the derivative that connects all humans, this beautiful one and only Earth we call home.

— Dey

mental health in the abstract until I began speaking to people in my community and listening to their stories. For women, many resort to drugs/alcohol to cope with abuse in the home, which can lead to PTSD. For men, I've noticed the result is due to PTSD, so there is a direct correlation to mental health.

I lost a very good friend of mine to substance abuse. We met in middle school and aged together. She was an only child, so she considered our friend group her sisters. I considered her to be my sister as well. Ours was a connection that remained strong no matter how far I traveled. As a direct result of depression and anxiety; I lost my dear friend that winter of 2018 to substance abuse and mental health problems. Mental health and substance abuse are very closely connected. As a community, we can not only heal ancestral pain but also our individual traumas through the use of our native medicine.

I used to work at the Mexican restaurant right above the lo'i kalo. There, I recognized a lot of men struggling with alcoholism. A lot of men hung out by the gate and drank beer while talking story. It lasted from the morning all the way until the evening. Sometimes it made me feel unsafe during the night hours, however; in daylight, I learned a lot of people, specifically of Micronesian descent, spoke of missing home and the aftereffects of Bikini Atoll. Embedded in substance abuse is a generational trauma, which is also a consequence of not having resources to address our mental health, generation after generation.

Some plants I would recommend in a community garden that address substance abuse would be 'Awa, Kī, and Hala. Each has its own healing properties, both physical and metaphysical. For example, Kī was used "to dispel evil, fresh leaves were worn around the neck, waist, and ankles and hung around dwellings. Masses were planted around homes to ward off evil and bring good fortune. It is a canoe crop, brought to the islands by the early Polynesians. Kī was considered sacred to the Hawaiian god, Lono, and to the goddess of the hula, Laka (Young). Pū Hala has emotional, spiritual, and nutritional value.

> Legend says that the hala tree is so abundant as a direct result of Pele's rage, whose canoe, on her first landing ashore, got entangled in the resistant roots and leaves. In her anger she ripped the trees in pieces and threw them across the island, and the hala sprouted, happy and wise, wherever it touched ground. Her anger was fortunate, because no other tree has been as useful to the Hawaiian people. From pollen to blossom to flower to fruit, from leaf to bark to wood to root, all parts had value (Schweitzer).

Hala root contains lots of vitamins B and C. Vitamin B helps with regulating folate in the brain, which in turn helps with depression. Vitamin B also aids cognitive development and memory functioning. Vitamin C helps with the feeling of being fatigued, and anyone who's ever been depressed knows that paired with feeling fatigued is a recipe for disaster and self-loathing.

If we use these herbs and plants correctly, we can develop a sense of accountability as we take control of our mental health. I think a big part of this accountability can be as simple as having a sign at the entrance, expressing the history of these plants and further aiding in cultural remembrance.

I think that the idea that holistic health is always considered pseudoscience and not as trustworthy, while pharmaceuticals are always considered effective and accessible is a false binary. Likewise, by utilizing the medicine of our ancestral medicine, we are directly resisting false binaries.

References

Perlas, Marjorie. "A History Of Kava Tea In Hawaii." Culture Trip, 2018, https://theculturetrip.com/north-america/usa/hawaii/articles/a-history-of-kava-in-hawaii/.

Schweitzer, Veronica. "The Hala Tree And The Art Of Lauhala." Coffeetimes. Com, 2006, http://www.coffeetimes.com/hala.htm.

Young, Peter. "Kī." Images Of Old Hawai'i, 2018, http://imagesofoldhawaii.com/ki/

Lyric B.

COMMUNITY IMPACT DESIGN PROJECT
Cultivating Black Joy

Goal: I will offer a youth-centered workshop that will highlight and cultivate Black joy and dreams through an afterschool club.

Addressing The Themes of Resistance:

Cultural Memory

Growing up, there was no representation of Black people in my dance community. It made me feel out of place, like I didn't fit in and this made me first realize that representation was extremely important. Not only was I not receiving the representation of people that looked like me but I was also not in an uplifting environment at home with my dreams in pursuing dance. I began to become unhappy in a place that I once considered a safe place and a home. This makes me want to create a safe space where others can share similar memories and their experiences of being isolated and not feeling "seen".

Countering Hegemony

In the context of dispossession and an overwhelming and limited narrative, this space would create spaces of opportunity, possibility, and affirmation by creating an afterschool club where the community affirms freedom of self-expression. where one is safe in Black expressions, joy, dreams, and an uplifting environment.

Accountability

During my time of doubt, instead of holding myself accountable and fighting through my troubles, I simply cowed away and quit dancing in a public studio and stuck to my bedroom. I don't want other kids, specifically Black/brown, shying away from their dreams simply because they don't feel comforted and loved in a community that's supposed to spread nothing but love. So not only should I hold myself accountable but those in authority (the teacher advisor) will be accountable for upholding the agreement that we have made while conducting the after school club. The club will be made not only by teachers but by students as well. Adults should hold themselves accountable in making sure that each and every kid there is happy and not feeling out of place.

Resisting False Binaries

Although I've been focusing on dance, I want to include all performing arts aspects into this after-school club. Movies that include Black people or Black stories are constantly talking about slavery or some form of racism needs to be apart of it, we are constantly reminded how this still occurs today when in reality everyone knows this story. Art is also supposed to be a safe place where people can forget about their worries.

After-school club activities would primarily focus on creating a safe space where Black youth don't feel the need to put up a front and let out all their emotions without judgment.

Strategy: Pillars of Liberation

Cultural Memory

1. **Institutions/Structures/people/communityorganizations:** The students and counselors/advisors at my high school will go over allyship training focused on what is appropriate and what isn't for the Black youth at school; creating a safe space for Black students to thrive just as much as their peers.
2. **Ideologies/Methodology/Education:** We will recognize that not only in these types of "Art" communities are Black kids usually left out. The ideology behind the after-school club is allowing Black youth to freely imagine and expand our possibilities in this world.
3. **Values/Behaviors/Belief/Empowerment:** I value my happiness along with my peers and I believe it should be just as important as those who aren't of Black descent. Instead of "dwelling" solely on mourning our ancestors, we can make them proud by creating new memories that are joyful and belong to us, allowing the youth that comes after us to be products of our joyful memories.

Countering Hegemony

1. **Institutions/Structures/people/community organizations:** Allow local musicians, artists, dancers, etc., to come into our organization as guests and connect with us during their time of visit. Although they are guests, the Black youth will have the authority to decide what will be allowed and what happens in the club.

2. **Ideologies/Methodology/Education:** Learning experiences will support culturally relevant values and artistry that will allow emotions to be shown.

3. **Values/Behaviors/Belief/Empowerment:** My after-school club will value diverse lived experiences and narratives in a judgment-free inclusive space. Participants will create and adhere to shared agreements.

Accountability

1. **Institutions/Structures/people/community organizations:** Myself, along with the participants, will hold each other accountable. If someone is giving off negative energy and something that doesn't resonate with love, comfortability, and joy, then we will have a talk and try to understand the root of the problem. How we handle conflict will be a part of a shared agreement that was created in the beginning.

2. **Ideologies/Methodology/Education:** Holding yourself accountable will teach you patience not only with yourself but with others.

3. **Values/Behaviors/Belief/Empowerment:** patience, love, kindness, joy, gentleness, and comfort

Resisting False Binaries

1. **Institutions/Structures/people/community organizations:** Oftentimes many institutions don't want to create a safe space. But if the false binaries that misrepresent Black youth come into play at my high school, the admin should be held accountable. And if the school does nothing to resolve the problem, the DOE will be contacted.

2. **Ideologies/Methodology/Education:** The youth in this program will not settle for anything less than other clubs in the school and we will demand to be treated with the same respect and decency. Not only physical safety but mental as well.

3. **Values/Behaviors/Belief/Empowerment:** We will not be taking any forms of racism, including microaggressions. We will continue to address these issues until someone puts a stop to it.

Noah Humphrey

COMMUNITY IMPACT DESIGN PROJECT

Holistic Healing:
A Repetition of Simpleness

I will offer a youth-centered workshop that will highlight and cultivate spiritual arts that will help those suffering through the stresses of
Covid-19 or other serious cases that have left a huge mark on their life. If
I heal myself, I heal my community because I have more energy to give
back rather than steal away. I want my mana, my energy, to be compati-
ble with those with generational trauma and to help them conquer their
inner demons and free themselves of a blockage that prevents them
from being a fully holistic person. These blockages consist of factors
such as a broken family, a broken heart, illness, setbacks, and failures,
which can become bad habits, walls, or doors of opportunity.

Countering Cultural Hegemony

Everyone can build as a healer, but not all can deconstruct their
trauma. No matter your identity, we all work toward healing the land.
To build a world where we can understand the power we have in the
joy in creating, the anger in destruction, and the bountifulness of the
lessons given to the land itself, we must introduce ourselves back to
the nature that forged us.

To have a group over a central person condenses and brings
harmony over the rule that could create different problems later. As
we solidify our being, demonstrate our inner soul of wellness, via self-
care and expand community service allying with the greater good, we
can break those structures that threaten to counter our claims to the
healing in which we effortlessly use for strength and compassion for
all. This space would counter cultural hegemony by creating spaces of
opportunity, possibility, and affirmation, via the facilitation of activities affirming freedom of self-expression via spiritual arts, (i.e. tai chi
for the community) direct energy healing by diverting trauma experiences, and other aspects to mentor and heal those in my vicinity and
most importantly in my community.

Accountability

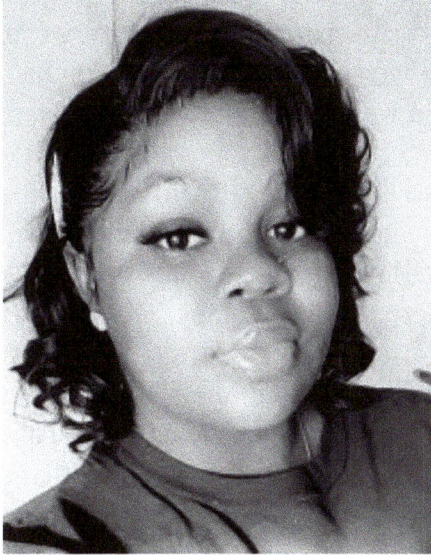

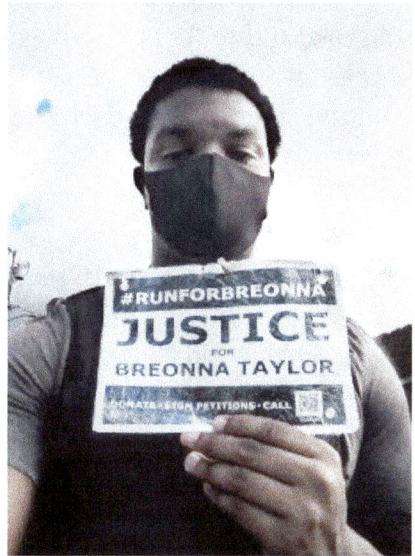

The accountability is doing the healing as it's instructed, from the past, and not to harm like the methods done by leaders before, but to heal. As I march, I understand that my actions create a movement. Her life is not in vain and from my walk and my activism I hold accountability for those who see this sign to say her name and for the community to gaze at my sign with the knowledge that she won't be erased. We cannot make haste with those treated with injustice lest we forget who we are as human beings. To be spiritual is to engage in a spiritual struggle. To be a healer you also have to enact on the injustice faced within your world

I want to change myself; I want to change my views on medicine and do my part to use this journey we call life to heal the community in which I inhabit. My education is subsidized in the theology of medicine. This all leads to the deeper source of who I prioritize with my values and the learnings of whom I give to in faith, customs, and the praxis my research steadily resides in. Tai chi is a way in which I express healing and my knowledge about medicinal plants; the capability in which I see ways to strengthen the land; and to converse with those of different beliefs to offer universal views of hope and faith. Essentially my ultimate goal is to complete this square within my life.

Resistance To False Binaries

The world is within the hands of the spirit of those willing to heal, to grow, and to feel the power within. No matter your identity, we all work toward healing the land. How we see our spirits, our conduct, and the style we approach the world we want to build are important factors to consider.

To break western imperialism, to promote equity, to prompt the liberty that provides us a chance to lead our resistance, we must open the gateways of our souls, thus increasing our levels of resistance. We must heal from the meditations that are falsely embodied within a patriarchal world.

Everyone can heal, and be a healer. Healing must displace the binary. We all can do the work that we need to heal. We have to be like the wave and crash through to the beat of our souls and soles until the land and the elements around brave through to embrace our clashes with life itself.

Questions for the reader:

1. What are the different pillars of oppression and LIBERATION that you can identify in my project?
2. What does a colonized home mean to you? What furniture would this place inhabit?

    Ex: A colonized home is a museum. The furniture would be artifacts of my people taken away from their native homelands

    Ex: A colonized home is a hotel, holding Ali'i trapped in glass for non-kanaka to see.

Acknowledgments

I have to start by thanking the Uli Movement's Weaving Our Stories participants: Ahmad, Aurora, Breena, Dey, Noah, and Lyric. We came together at the start of a dangerous and isolating global pandemic and witnessed the intensification of hate and violence against our bodies and bodies like ours. We leaned into one another and found a way to dream and build amidst this overwhelming pain. I have 100% faith that your stories and your brave voices are the healing balm the world needs now.

I want to thank the artists and authors, mentors, and community supporters whose work is featured here in the *Weaving Our Stories: Return To Belonging* Anthology. This collection would have been impossible without the gift of your resistance story. I thank each of you for your vulnerability, trust, and the unique lens you brought to *Weaving Our Stories*. To our community supporters in Hawaiʻi and beyond, I thank you for trusting us to learn from and share your brilliance, resistance, and vision for a more just and liberated world. This work is a kākou thing!

Throughout this work, I have called on my family, the communities that hold me, my circle of sister-friends, my ancestors, and the land I call home, Hawaiʻi. I would not have had the capacity nor clarity of vision needed for this project were it not for your wisdom and love. When I found myself unsure of my purpose and direction, I called on my Great Grandmother, the trailblazing suffragist, educator, and community organizer, Frances Berry Coston. When I have felt out of place, unwanted, I have called on her daughter, my Grandmother, the prodigal Black classical pianist and teacher, Jean Coston. I have also called on the island warrior who navigated new and unwelcoming spaces with tenacity and grace, my Grandmother, Afriquita Lapuz. I have called on my rebellious and always truth-telling Mother, Bootsy Deese when I needed to bring the fire. I thank each of my seven siblings and my children, a beautiful rainbow tribe that continues to inspire me and hold me accountable to what matters most in this life– love. Malaika and Pono, being your mother has been the most enlightening lesson in love and accountability I've ever encountered. You've shown me the true function and power of honesty, the importance of deep listening, and the indispensable need for playfulness in this often somber world. My five sisters, Jade, Lani, Domo, Charis, and Sophie, thank you for shaking me up when I forget who I am, and who we are. To my two warrior brothers, Clint and Stephan, one day the world will know your story and you will see your reflection, and you will see what we see– beautiful men, worthy of love. We are pretty dang awesome. Last, but never least, thank you, Pūlama Long, for co-creating the vision and direction of Weaving Our Stories. Thank you for your friendship, trust, and shared commitment to radical resistance and accountability to this beautiful place I am lucky to call home.

Meet Our Community Storytellers

Luanna Peterson advocates for self-determination as an organizer and a community educator. She co-founded Weaving Our Stories, a Hawai'i-rooted abolitionist program focused on storytelling as a means of liberation. Luanna is an inaugural Peace Studio Fellow and Director of Learning and Evaluation at Mothering Justice, a policy advocacy organization that provides mothers of color with resources to use their power to impact policy. She has extensive experience creating, managing, and delivering place and culture-based community programs. Her career has centered on community empowerment and sustainability through education and advocacy. She loves to engage her community in deeper learning, better preparing them for success and the most important parts of life: being an empowered individual.

Co-Founder **Pūlama Long** was born and raised in Washington. At 18 years old, she returned to her ancestral lands, Hawai'i. Pūlama received her Bachelor of Arts degree from the Kamakakūokalani Center for Hawaiian Studies at the University of Hawai'i and, in 2020, graduated with a teaching certificate from Kaho'iwai. Pūlama is a cultural practitioner who teaches lauhala weaving in the community.

Weaving Our Stories Ancestral Guide: **Nana Sula** was initiated in Ghana, West Africa, in 2007 at the Shrine of Impohema and has studied the mysteries of Ghana since 1992. Her initiation title is Nana Okomfo Kokwe Ama Tawiah. Nana Sula has also studied Ifa/Orisha mysteries of Nigeria since 1985. In 2014, Sula Spirit authored and produced

the Book and CD project entitled *Spirit of the Orisha*. This Yoruba language preservation project is a 38-track CD in the Yoruba language with a matching book of translations. Sula is also an instructor of sacred music and travels globally to teach Orisha and Ghanaian chants. She was born and raised in New Jersey and has been a New Orleans, LA resident since 1996. Nana Sula Spirit credits all she is to the Father and Mother of Creation, her parents, grandparents, the Orisha, Abusom, and Ancestors. She is a singer/songwriter with her own worldbeat band Coin-Coin and recently recorded her debut solo CD in Tanzania, East Africa, entitled *A Journey Within*. Sula is also the lead singer of Mojuba, an Orisha, Afro-Cuban band, and The Maroons, an African conga and shekere trio based in New Orleans, Louisiana.

Weaving our Stories Mentors, Community Speakers, and Our Supporters

Youth Mentor **Manulani Aluli Meyer** is a cultural practitioner coming home after 25 years in Hilo and five years in Aotearoa, New Zealand. She is a worldwide Indigenous scholar dedicated to expanding views of epistemology to address the needs of our time better.

Youth Mentor **Imani Altemus-Williams** was raised in Honolulu, Hawai'i, and is a Sámi University of Applied Sciences graduate. She received her master's degree in Indigenous Journalism. With genealogical ties to what is now known as Louisiana, she wrote her thesis on the interrelation between storytelling and resistance for Black & Native peoples protecting Louisiana's sacred lands. Along

with freelance writing and co-producing two documentaries, Imani is passionate about gathering stories that illustrate the collective experiences of colonized peoples by highlighting not only injustice, trauma, and pain but also our inherent resilience, strength, and beauty.

Youth Mentor **Danyale Thomas** integrates connection, collaboration, and celebration to encourage women through life's transitions. This integration was the driving force behind her 25-year career in the beauty industry and helped form her commitment to finding ways to serve her community meaningfully. From 2018-2019, Danyale was the enthusiastic leader of the Honolulu WomanSpeak circle. WomanSpeak focuses on educating, supporting, and uplifting its members, resulting in a woman developing her message and using her voice to change the world. Danyale is also certified as a Rapid Transformation Therapy™ Practitioner. RTT offers unparalleled results by combining the most beneficial principles of hypnotherapy, NLP, psychotherapy, and cognitive behavioral therapy. Most recently, Danyale has partnered her entrepreneurial background, passion, and commitment to uplifting women with the strength and resources of New York Life Insurance company as a financial services professional.

Youth Mentor **Brianna Mims** is an artist, abolitionist, and facilitator from Jacksonville, Florida, based in Los Angeles, CA. She has trained and performed in many different dance forms for several years. Her work, which spans the disciplines of fashion, dance, advocacy, facilitation, curation, and direction, is rooted in self and cultural explorations, healing, and shifting culture alongside policy to create sustainable change. She experiences the body as a site of liberation and uses that information

to guide organizing, facilitating, and all of the art she creates. Mims graduated from the University of Southern California, where she studied Dance, NGOs, and Social Change. She currently works for Californians United for a Responsible Budget and is a Toulmin Fellow. You can find her at www.bjmims.com.

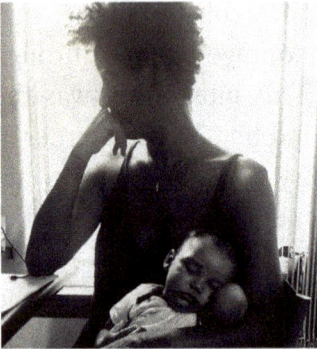

Youth Mentor **Piper Lovemore** is a midwife, doula, birth educator, and community birth worker. Piper Lovemore's work is focused on cultivating community empowerment through traditional birth work. Centered around inspiring people to honor and trust Intuition, her approach is rooted in the principles of Universal Love, Transcendent Mutuality, and nurturing the deep-seated confidence that is their natural by-product. She lives in Hawai'i with her partner and their seven unschooled children.

Youth Mentor **Danielle Atkinson** has extensive experience as a church-based, electoral, and community organizer. She has worked with organizations such as America Votes, State Voices, Population Connection, and ACORN. In 2012, Atkinson founded Mothering Justice, a leadership development and advocacy organization. Atkinson has organized efforts to raise the minimum wage in Florida and Michigan. Mothering Justice also fought to earn paid sick time in Michigan. Her work organizing mothers won her the 2013 Michigan Organizer of the Year Award. Atkinson received bachelor's degrees in political science and sociology from Pfeiffer University.

Youth Mentor **Joshlyn Noga** was born and raised in Kalihi, O'ahu. She is 27 years old and an 8th-grade 'āina based educator at King Intermediate School on the island's windward side. Although it has been ten years since she last lived in Kalihi, Kalihi will always live in her. More than just her hometown, Kalihi is where all her ancestors first

settled when they moved to O'ahu. Kalihi is her piko to O'ahu. Kalihi is woven into my family's story of coming together. She is a proud Hawaiian, Black, and Samoan woman.

Youth Mentor **M. Malia Connor** is the founder and artistic director of the Oakland-based dance group "Malia Movement Company," the author of four books (poetry, a children's book, and photography) and a featured poet in two publications, "Black Fathers, An Invisible Presence In America" with her father and "Namjai," a collection of AAPI artists from the greater Bay Area.

Video Editor and Community Speaker **Summer Bowie** is the managing editor of *Autre Magazine*, an LA-based art and fashion publication online and in print. As a former dancer and educator, she brings her studies in movement and language to her assessment of culture.

Community Speaker **Kinohi Fukumitzu** is a mother of four children, a fishpond practitioner, a writer, and is obsessed with 'āina. She is very sensitive to energy and the energy exchanged between people and 'āina. She believes this energy exchange will heal the world and nourish our minds, bodies, and spirits. She has a BA in Hawaiian Studies. She has spent more than a decade learning from He'eia Fishpond and has moved to bring the skills and

knowledge to her community in her hometown of Waimānalo. From sharing her skillset of wall building as a woman to protecting ʻiwi kupuna at Hūnānāniho and Hakipuʻu she has gone against the grain with ʻāina being at the forefront of what moves her.

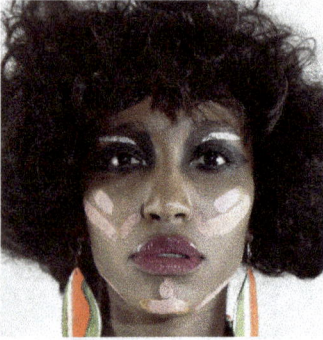

Community Speaker **Lexie Lechelt** of THIS IS Black: They say having a child changes you and having a daughter profoundly impacted Lexie. From conception, she immediately thought about her freedom, happiness, and development. She doesn't want her daughter to be saddled with limitations and suffocating negative stereotypes often imposed on Black people growing up in Western societies and/or former colonies. So, she founded THIS IS Black as a space to learn about Black people from other Black people. THIS IS Black is a space to feel comfortable in all of our Blackness, regardless of your shade, socioeconomic background, or country. In his book *Between The World and Me*, Ta-Nehisi Coates writes, "You are growing into consciousness, and my wish for you is that you feel no need to constrict yourself to make other people comfortable." #Blackisbeautiful

Community Speaker **Marie Eriel Hobro** is a Filipina documentary photographer, journalist, filmmaker, and educator based on Oʻahu, Hawaiʻi. She was born in Maryland (DC area) and raised between Mililani and Wahiawa in Hawaiʻi. She received her Bachelor of Science in Visual Journalism from Brooks Institute and attended the Eddie Adams XXIX Workshop as a student in the fall of 2016. She is also a Women Photograph, Diversify Photo, and Authority Collective member, running the visual storytelling collective Wolf & Woman. Her work is deeply rooted in her passion for dismantling

the stereotypes associated with Hawai'i. As a bisexual woman of color, she is particularly drawn to stories celebrating individuality, identity, BIWOC, and the LGBTQ+ community. When she's not working, she can be found obsessing over roller skating and pretending like she's a discount ballerina on wheels.

Community Speaker **Tito Romero** is the co-founder and outreach coordinator for Flowers & Bullets Collective. He was born in Tucson and is a lifelong resident of Barrio Centro. As community organizers, Tito and Flowers & Bullets have been instrumental in using food and art to address intersectionality around issues like mass incarceration, food insecurity, and affordable housing. By using the land and place-based connections, we're here to redefine what public safety really means.

WOS Logo Design Artist **Cassandra Chee** (she/her) is a printmaker, organizer, and follower of Jesus, who resists cis White hetero-patriarchy. She holds a Bachelor of Visual Communications Design from the University of Washington and a Master of Divinity from Garrett–Evangelical Theological Seminary. While her roots run through Korea, China, and Okinawa, she has been a settler on the lands of the Duwamish, Chumash, and in the Hawaiian Kingdom. As a fourth-generation displaced settler in Hawai'i, Cassie is committed to co-creating and building power with the people and 'āina that has nourished her family for a more just world.

Community Supporter: The **Hawaii Community Bailfund** is a proud member of the National Bail Fund Network, a national project that works with organizers, advocates, and legal providers across the country

HAWAII
COMMUNITY
BAIL
FUND

that are using, or contemplating using, community bail funds as part of efforts to change local bail systems and reduce incarceration radically.

Community Supporter: **First Unitarian Church Of Honolulu** believes that they realize their Unitarian Universalist Principles most fully in a compassionate, just, and joyous community, and that the vigorous diversity of their church must also work in unity to fulfill their mission. The First Unitarian Church Of Honolulu models an effective and responsible social justice ministry in the world. As a church, their social justice ministry feels most effective when they focus on the spiritual and root causes of injustice whenever possible. Their social justice leadership style is collegial, consultative, inclusive, and principle-based rather than issue-oriented – issues invite factions, and principles invite community!

Community Supporter: The **Shanti Alliance** is a Stevens World Peace Foundation Program, launched in the Fall of 2020 to equip students and educators with the knowledge and skills necessary to be effective diversity, equity, and inclusion practitioners. Learning from expert practitioners and each other, students develop school action projects to improve their school communities, with students & faculty developing and broadening their skills to facilitate conversations surrounding topics related to diversity, equity, inclusion, and belonging. (shantialliance.org)

Community Supporter: **It's Lit with PhDJ** features writers to love and the music their work plays best around. Born in November 2016 on KTUH as a radio show, It's Lit is now a podcast that features poets, spoken word artists, musical performers, flash fiction and creative nonfiction writers, and more. So the lit is literature, and it's lit because it's awesome. The show has a soft spot for women-of-color writers, Indigenous writers, LGBTQI+ writers, intersectional writers, the-personal-is-political writers, ally-is-a-verb writers, drawing-on-our-ancestors writers, heart-wrenching writers, the-revolution-won't-be-televised writers, sexy writers, boundary-exploding writers, healing writers, community-building writers, damn-the-man-and-the-empire writers, all-of-the-above writers—along with love for a strange mix of genre-bending music. Connect with the show on Instagram @itslitwithphdj and online at www.itslitwithphdj.wordpress.com.

Weaving our Stories
Youth Series Youth Organizers

Deysha Childs is an aspiring renaissance woman. She would love to categorize herself as an astrophysicist, but she loves so much more than that. Although that is her preferred field of study. For now, she models and works as a waitress.

Noah Humphrey goes by the stage name Knowa-Know; pronouns are he-series. He is in a Master of Divinity Program and recently graduated from Whittier College with a BA in Religious Studies and a minor in Holistic Care. He uses poetry as his second voice and infuses his experiences in South Central; his African-American heritage; neo spirituality, nature; and holistic elements into his art. He lets his soul speak through poetry and believes that with peace, passion, patience, support, and God, anything

is possible through this path we call life. You can find Knowa-Know on IG @knowaknow, the blog platform Mirakee @knowaknow, and via Linktree at https://linktr.ee/knowaknow.

Ahmad Selim Aboagye Xallen uses he/him pronouns. He loves plants, cooking, and dancing. He is on a journey to learn more about medicine, how to use a bow and arrow, and how to better love the parts of himself that he is embarrassed about. His Instagram is @AxAboagye.

Aurora Jeffrey is a lifelong learner in work and life. As an educator, her goal is to empower kids to listen to their bodies, ask questions about norms, and encourage community. These are natural inclinations young kids have! She uses those inclinations to facilitate conversations about real-world issues in age-appropriate ways. Aurora owes her growth to Hilo, where she was raised, Poughkeepsie, where she began her own empowering, and Huichin, CA (commonly known as Richmond) where she lives now.

Breena Thompson is from Hawthorne California. She is currently pursuing a marine bology and ethnic studies degree. She would love to make a change she'll be remembered for. Ultimately, she wants to positively impact the world we live in.

Lyric B: Our youngest youth series participant is a talented high school student who enjoys and excels in the arts and academics. She is a singer-songwriter, and dancer and loves to bring joy to her friends. She hopes to create a safe space for Black youth to find joy in the arts in an environment free of judgment and racism.

Weaving Our Stories Spring Resistance Anthology Writers and Artists

Alisha Kahealani Mahone-Brooks, born on the island of Oʻahu, is deeply rooted in her Kanaka Maoli heritage. Her connection to her lāhui (people) and ʻāina (land) is a commitment she holds close to her heart. By dedicating herself to the land, her people, and the Creator, Kahealani continues to strengthen and celebrate her heritage. Her connection is evident in her embrace of the Hawaiian language, her dedication to learning the names and stories of places and people, and her expression of love and care towards them. This profound relationship anchors her to her roots, reminding her of the importance of connections in a world that often feels disconnected. The pride Kahealani takes in her heritage stems from the deep relational nature of her people, serving as a guiding force in a world craving genuine connection. She believes her heritage is fundamentally about nurturing - caring for people, the Earth, and all living beings. This belief and love for all creation are at the core of her being. Follow Kahealani's journey at @kahea.mana.hina.

Amy Benson is a Nigerian-American creative entrepreneur based in Honolulu, Hawaiʻi. Birthed to Nigerian parents, she was born in Anniston, Alabama, and grew up in Birmingham, Alabama. Benson attended college at the University of Alabama, and finished her Bachelor of Arts degree at the University of Texas, San Antonio. After graduation, she began her professional career in Atlanta, Georgia working in industries such as marketing, sales, and luxury hospitality. In 2013, Benson relocated to Honolulu, Hawaiʻi and over the course of 7 years, worked in aviation, consulting, Human Resources, and hospitality before founding her company Afro Aloha. Afro Aloha is Hawaiʻi's cultural hub for black locals and travelers which focuses on connecting people through art, culture, entrepreneurship, and wellness. Benson is also the creator and host of The Afro Aloha Podcast.

APRIL LAWRENCE

Alejandra Alexander is an intersection of many experiences. She uses art and writing to capture moments, things, people, and experiences that bring her joy and healing. She uses writing and photography to find clarity and meaning in the human experiences that sometimes leave her confused

KIM TODD

and ashamed. Her art holds all the pieces together as she seeks to become fully whole. You can glean that in her work @ChironConjunctSunInGemini

"Good trouble" is a driving force in **Allison Jacobs**' life, shaping her quest for justice that isn't focused on "just us." This passion led to her legal studies at the University of California, Berkeley. Allison exists in alternate realities: fighting for social justice and antiracism daily and writing fantasy and romance by night. Her story, I am Not the Nanny, written under Cora Cooper, appeared in *Chicken Soup for the Soul: I'm Speaking Now: Black Women Share Their Truth in 101 Stories of Love, Courage, and Hope.*

Cassandra Chee (she/her) is rooted in Okinawa, Korea, and China. She was raised on Duwamish land (Kirkland, WA), and her family has been settlers in Hawai'i since plantation times.

David Akeo is an island-born educator and artist who studied in Las Vegas, Nevada. His diverse skill sets have taken him from the regular classroom to the outdoors as an environmental and native Hawaiian cultural educator. He also worked in curriculum development and illustrated plants, animals, and traditional ways of life for educational publications. All of his works for this project were done using Microsoft Paint. He designed the logos for each of our chapters of resistance for this volume: cultural memory, accountability, countering hegemony and resisting false binaries.

Demiliza Sagaral Saramosing is an educator, scholar, and teaching artist of Bisayan descent with genealogies rooted in the seas shared between the Visayas and Mindanao. She was born and raised in the

U.S. racial capitalist and occupying settler state of Hawai'i. She grew up a Filipina deep in the heart of Kalihi, an ahupua'a, and an urban neighborhood of Honolulu. Demiliza attributes her passion for justice to her experiences growing up in Kalihi and her time studying, learning from, and engaging in political movements in Hawai'i, Oregon, California, and Minnesota. She is currently a Ph.D. candidate at the University of Minnesota's American studies program located in occupied Dakota homelands. If you are interested in connecting with Demiliza, please follow her on Instagram @bisayanremix or Twitter @WadingMess.

Gabriel Verduzco is originally from Sacramento, California. Gabriel came to Hawai'i to attend UH Mānoa. Gabriel is an American Studies major with a focus in Indigenous knowledge, history, and political & social issues. Gabriel discovered their passion for writing. Check out Gabriel's poems and a life story essay @papichulo.verduzco.

Gillian Dueñas tells her stories through visual art. She explores her identity as a mixed-race Indigenous Pacific Islander woman born and raised in the diaspora by painting, weaving, carving, and jewelry making. Her art is an act of reclamation, decolonization, and healing. She takes inspiration from traditional motifs, legends, and jewelry and reimagines them in a modern context. Overall, she uses art to amplify her stories as well as the stories of my community.

Jade Rhodes is an aspiring urban ecologist/designer and environmental justice advocate born in Detroit, MI, and now living on O'ahu. As an Afro-indigenous woman, her perspective and frustrations of being disconnected from the land her ancestors were stolen from and the land that was stripped from under them simultaneously have guided her principles of thinking about how we can reconnect with place, land, and culture, through flora and fauna as a vehicle of healing.

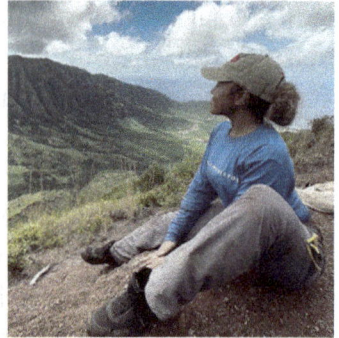

Jess Heard is an anti-racist facilitator and truth-teller. She writes poetry and

prose, performs stand-up comedy, and shares eclectic expressions of resistance and liberation on Instagram @TheWilling4.

Joshlyn Noga was born and raised in Kalihi, Oʻahu. She is 27 years old and an 8th-grade ʻāina based educator at King Intermediate School located on the island's Windward side. Although it has been ten years since she last lived in Kalihi, Kalihi will always live in her. More than just her hometown, Kalihi is where all of her ancestors first settled when they moved to Oʻahu. Kalihi is her piko to Oʻahu. Kalihi is woven into her family's story of coming together. She is a proud Hawaiian, Black, and Samoan

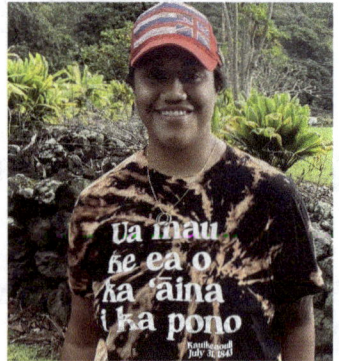

woman.

Kealohilani Minami (she/they) is a Queer Femme artist passionate about food sovereignty and decolonization through everyday acts of resistance. Reclaiming the Hana Noʻeau cultural practice of making lei in Denver (CO), they educate people about Native Hawaiian politics and history

through community markets and social media (@Lei by Kealohi). They also spend time in mutual aid around food access, freelance DEI consulting, and developing her relationship with the 'āina while pursuing a degree in Political Science at UH Mānoa. She hopes to connect with others through art, believing it's an intimate space for pushing the boundaries of our world, (un)learning, & activation. IG @ mskealohi

Karima Daoudi is the proud daughter of Kristin Lems and Abdelkader Daoudi and the proud granddaughter of Carol Lems-Dworkin, Willem Lems, Ahmed Daoudi, and Halima Zidouk. She was born and raised in Evanston, Illinois on the shores of Lake Michigan in the ancestral lands of the Potawatomi, Miami, Peoria, and Oceti Sakowin people. She currently resides in Honolulu in the occupied Kingdom of Hawai'i. Karima embodies Amazigh, Arab, Dutch, German, British, and Jewish heritages. She identifies as North African, Algerian, American, and a Chicagoan but also acknowledges that no racial and ethnic categories created under a structure of white supremacy can tell the full stories of our humanity. She also has hānai (adoptive) family in both Fiji and Senegal, who have greatly influenced her life and the person she is. Karima is an educator, cultural producer, and artist who strives to center social justice, racial equity, and global citizenship creatively and collaboratively. Her early life strongly influenced Karima's values and interests, which provided a foundation of activism, internationalism, and music via her mother, a feminist folk singer/songwriter; her grandmother, a concert pianist and activist; and her Dutch grandfather and Algerian father. She loves to create art, play music, and be in nature.

Kuʻuleianuhea Awo-Chun is a kanaka ʻōiwi mother, educator, and author from Koʻolaupoko, Oʻahu. She is passionate about social justice, Real Housewives, and french fries. She graduated from Kailua High School, the University of Puget Sound, and UH Mānoa, MedT, and has worked in Hawaiian-Focused Charter Schools for over two decades.

Lauren Ballesteros-Watanabe is a third-generation Mexican- American Chicana raised by a single mother. She is a storyteller, filmmaker, vegan, mother, and environmental justice organizer with the Sierra Club of Hawaiʻi. Her proudest achievement is healing through motherhood, decolonizing parenting, and raising a multi-racial daughter with intention and unconditional love. You can check her out at @laur4paz

Lesley G Harvey is a dedicated community organizer and activist. Professionally, Lesley is a long-time grant writer and non-profit/small business consultant. Focused on social justice through collective action, Lesley aims to galvanize critical mass to bring about change and is active in areas of equity justice. You can find her on Instagram @ellle.geee.

Mariana Aqʼabʼal Moscoso (they/them/theirs) is a nonbinary indigenous Queer of detribalized Achi Mayan and Afro-indigenous roots living in unceded Nisanan land. They are a child of a courageous mother and a solo parent of a creative daughter. A budding healer and liberation doula that creates art that centers on decolonization and Mayan cosmovision. Mariana is a storyteller, digital

artist, graphic designer, and zine maker. They are a co-visionary of Toj + Tijax: The Ritual of Myth Making, an indigenous queer healing space, and working as the Arts in Corrections Program Manager at the California Arts Council. www.ritualofmythmaking.com

Navjeet Kaur is an interdisciplinary artist whose art practice is based on preserving the stories of those that came before her through somatic remembrance of ancestral practices such as weaving, movement, breathwork, and ritual traditions based in reimagined mythologies. She explores concepts of harmony and chaos existing within the body, spirit, and earth through maternal connections, identity, home, and belonging. Being from a Punjabi-Sikh family and identifying as that herself, she feels it is important to address topics of intergenerational trauma and resilience through remembering in her work. Kaur currently lives and works in Detroit, Michigan. Instagram: navjeetkaurrr – Website: https://www.navjeetkaurart.com/

Nikki Depriest is a visual artist and advocate for arts education in the Portland area who works in ink, watercolors, and oils to convey an expression of whimsical beauty, often portraying the experiences of Black and indigenous folx with a heavy focus on self-care practices and joy. It was her investment in her own arts education, where she received her degree in New York, further studying painting techniques in Italy, the Caribbean islands, and various communities within Turtle Island, that continued to inform her how creating art is an ultimate bridge builder.

Pumehana Cabral is a proud Kanaka ʻŌiwi whose life centers around social justice & community building – specifically with other

māhū and BIPOC folks. Pumehana runs its own business encompassing journalism, documentary film production, ʻāina-based education, and creative project management. They believe collaborative, and creative work is pivotal to long-term social change in Hawaiʻi and beyond.

Share Roman is a Black & South Asian Caribbean (dougla), neurodivergent poet, community organizer, and DEI consultant. Share has developed and led LGBTQIA+ and DEI-based curricula, workshops, training, and community spaces in New York City, NY, USA, and the Kingdom of Hawaiʻi. Share works through the lenses of accessibility, diversity, intentional solidarity, inclusion, and anti-respectability politics.

Val Guevarra is an artist using recycled/upcycled plastic medicine caps for mosaics, pointillists, portraits, images, and figures. He noticed that colorful plastic medicine caps were being thrown away and not being recycled or reused! So, he began collecting them and turning them into colorful mosaic art. It is up to the viewer to discern the image or connect the dots (pun intended).

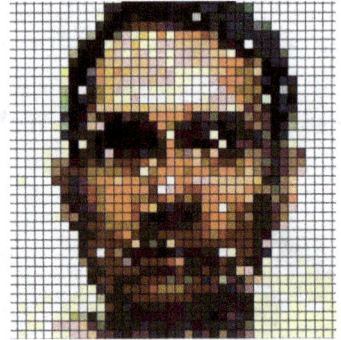

Whether or not the work is understood is up to the audience. One can enjoy the abstract colors of the plastic caps up close or discover the hidden images from a distance! Hue are what hue see(k)!- Separ8tor

AN UNYIELDING TRUTH:
A MANIFESTO FOR GLOBAL LIBERATION

Luanna Peterson, Co-Founder of Weaving Our Stories

The life of the land and her people are worthy, everywhere and always. The thousands of innocent Palestinian children whose cries pierce the night as bombs destroy their homes are worthy. The victims of the Maui fires, who continue to suffer in the aftermath of disaster capitalism, are worthy. The waters and land of Oʻahu, tainted by the U.S. military-industrial complex, are worthy. The Congolese, who endure unimaginable horrors as wealthy nations steal their minerals so the world can obsess over gadgets, are worthy. These are not just isolated tragedies; they are symptoms of a global crisis rooted in disregarding the intrinsic worth of life and land in favor of imagined narratives rooted in racism and political and economic hegemony.

Recognizing the worth of all people – the seen and unseen, the forgotten and remembered, the dead and the yet-to-be-born – is crucial not only as a moral imperative but also as a means to safeguard our collective well-being, preserve the integrity of our land, and protect our mental and spiritual health. Ignoring this truth has had far-reaching and long-lasting consequences, leading to a world marred by violence, the degradation of the land that sustains all of us, and a pervasive sense of despair and disconnection. By committing to actions that uphold this unchanging truth, we can awaken from this destructive cycle, fostering a world that respects and protects the dignity and well-being of all life.

The U.S. has a vested interest in maintaining false narratives that justify illegal occupation, puppet governments, and the sale of military equipment globally. These interests, driven by power and greed, overshadow the intrinsic worth of life and land. But in a world where economic and geopolitical interests often dominate, I stand firm in my commitment to the truth of our worth. Recognizing our immutable worth is the first step toward genuine liberation and justice.

Imagine a world where our policies and practices reflect the intrinsic value of every person and the land they inhabit, where sustainable development and peace are not mere ideals but lived realities. Where communities are empowered, and their voices shape the decisions that affect their lives.

To achieve this, we need more than individual commitment; we need collective action. Societies and communities must work together to implement policies and practices that honor and protect the dignity of all life and the sanctity of our planet. Sure, economic growth and stability are paramount for our collective prosperity, but economic development at the expense of human rights and environmental sustainability is fundamentally flawed. Prosperity built on suffering and exploitation leads to societal divisions and long-term instability. The situations in Hawai'i where I am now, and in Palestine, Sudan, and the Congo serve as stark examples of where occupation of sovereign land and resource exploitation has resulted in extensive human suffering and displacement.

Let us carry with us not only the awareness of the challenges we face but also a sense of hope and possibility. The vision of a world where every life and every piece of land is respected is not just a dream; it is an attainable reality if we join forces and commit to this path. Our collective actions, grounded in the recognition of our shared worth, have the power to transform our world. May we all be inspired to weave these truths into the fabric of our daily lives, and may our actions reflect the unyielding truth of our collective worth. Together, we will continue to strive for a world of freedom, justice, equality, and dignity for all.

Consider Palestine, where, as I write this, genocide rages. In the Gaza Strip, the grim reality of over 15,000 Palestinians lost, including more than 6,150 children since October 2023[1], starkly illustrates the urgent need to reassess our global priorities. This ongoing siege, often rationalized as necessary for self-defense, is less a matter of security and more a manifestation of a distorted global narrative. If we extend our gaze back to 1948, to the onset of the Zionist occupation, the scale

---

1 Al Jazeera. (2023, November 27). Israel-Hamas War Live: Calls to Extend Truce Grow as Captives Released. Al Jazeera. Retrieved 27 November 2023 from https://www.aljazeera.com/news/liveblog/2023/11/27/israel-hamas-war-live-calls-to-extend-truce-grow-as-captives-released

of the tragedy becomes even more apparent. Yet, the focus often remains narrowly fixated on Hamas. This selective attention serves the interests of those who benefit from the status quo, enabling the perpetuation of falsehoods that obscure a painful yet undeniable truth: the unceasing disregard of the Palestinians' immutable worth in pursuit of power and profit.

Similarly, the Sudanese genocide, driven by international interests in oil, has led to the death of 9,000 people and the displacement of 5.6 million[2], revealing the catastrophic consequences of prioritizing profits over people. U.S. and European companies and investors actively engage in various economic activities in Sudan, primarily securing oil and other essential natural resources. Managing these resources and their revenues are major factors in the Sudanese conflict, resulting in the worthy deemed disposable and money being elevated to god status.

At present, there is also a genocide taking place in the Congo. The millions of displaced and countless murdered in the Congo are also more worthy than the resources that power our newest devices. The United States' engagement in the Democratic Republic of Congo (DRC) primarily focuses on economic gains, particularly in the mining sectors of cobalt and coltan, which are essential for electronics. This pursuit significantly influences local dynamics, often exacerbating conflicts over these valuable resources. The DRC's tormented history, marked by colonialism and foreign interference – notably the US-backed assassination of the democratically elected Patrice Lumumba and the subsequent installation of Mobutu Sese Seko – continues to have profound and lasting effects. The ongoing unrest serves Western corporate interests in the region's minerals, often supported by military backing from Western nations. If we shift the narrative to acknowledge that, while these resources are worthwhile, they should not be valued above human lives, it could lead to reevaluating how these resources are obtained and managed.

2 Ahmed, Kaamil and Mohammed Salih, Zeinab. "Sudan's cycle of violence: 'There is a genocide going on in West Darfur'." The Guardian, 21 Nov. 2023, [https://www.theguardian.com/global-development/2023/nov/21/sudans-cycle-of-violence-there-is-a-genocide-going-on-in-west-darfur]

The plight of regions like Palestine, Sudan, and the Congo, where exploitation and disregard for human life are rampant, urgently calls for a reevaluation of our global priorities. It is imperative that our relationships evolve from exploitation to nurturing, acknowledging the inherent worth of every individual and the land that sustains us. This shift is not just a lofty aspiration but a critical necessity. The global negligence of the immutable worth of our land and its people carries deep mental and spiritual consequences. The pervasive violence and dehumanization sow seeds of despair, particularly among younger generations, who are acutely aware of the formidable challenges they are set to inherit. We must realize that although global powers may overlook the significance of our collective worth, the united voice of the masses refuses to be silenced. With time, we have the power to overturn the false narratives that have long restrained humanity, ushering in an era of justice and truth through our shared resolve.

In Hawai'i, where I write these words, we also render the worthy, including ourselves, invisible. The U.S. continues to occupy the sovereign nation of Hawai'i, and everyday white supremacist institutions fuel division among marginalized communities because our oppressor does not acknowledge our immutable worth. Societal binaries are evident in the oversimplified narrative of 'us versus them' or 'good versus evil,' often portrayed in media coverage and social media commentary on domestic and international conflicts. But correcting the narrative begins even closer to home; it starts with me.

I will counter these obstacles by telling those who do not see me that I have been here all along. I will remind you that my grandparents' brilliance laid the foundation for a universal culture that refuses to recognize its forbearers. My ancestors life-affirming ideas and their many contributions to humanity changed the world even if you now take that brilliance for granted, even if you somehow imagined that their gifts of belonging, intellect, culture, language, music, and medicine fell from the sky from an anonymous source just for you. I will speak to my wounded inner child, who grew up in Waipahu under the shadows of US racism and capitalist occupation, affirming our inherent worth that was overlooked. I will address the painful exclusion from my family, rooted in their inability to embrace my Blackness and assert my rightful place in our shared history.

Moreover, I will echo this affirmation of worth and belonging for Hawai'i, Palestine, Congo, Sudan, and all the oppressed and invisible peoples across the globe. Their contributions, often unseen and unacknowledged, have enriched our world in ways immeasurable and profound. It is time their stories, their struggles, and their triumphs are brought to light and given the recognition they so rightfully deserve.

In closing, to those who disregard my immutable worth: We have been fighting side-by-side for our collective freedom for generations, even as you ask: what have you or your people done for me or my people? I forgive you for not seeing across artificial boundaries of me versus you, us versus them, for forgetting that I would live and die for the truth. I will live and die for a Free Palestine. I will live and die for a Free Hawai'i. I will live and die for the life of the land and her people everywhere. I forgive you for not witnessing my pain when you are pained. I forgive you for not believing my life mattered because I am something other than you. I forgive you because my worth and yours are intertwined and immutable, and this truth cannot be altered.

Free Hawa'ii, Free Palestine, Free Congo, Free Sudan.
Free West Papua. Free the Black, Brown, and Indigenous
of so-called America. Free All Oppressed Peoples Everywhere.

Works Cited

"Ancient Moku & Ahupua'a". Maui Nui Ahupua'a Project. https://www.mauinui-ahupuaaproject.com/ahupuaa. Accessed 27 March 2022.

"Mo'olelo: Keahiakahoe." https://www.hookuaaina.org/mo%CA%BBolelo-keahiakahoe/. Accessed 27 March 2022.

Goodyear-Ka'ōpua, Noelani, et al. "Teaching Amid U.S. Occupation: Sovereignty, Survival, and Social Studies in a Native Hawaiian Charter School." Kamehameha Schools, Hūlili: Multidisciplinary Research on Hawaiian Well-Being, 2008, p 178, https://kamehamehapublishing.org/wp-content/uploads/sites/38/2020/09/Hulili_Vol5_5.pdf. Accessed 3 March 2022

Hofschneider, Anita. HPD Chief Says There's Less Racial Bias In Hawaii. She's Wrong." *Civil Beat*, 29 June 2020, https://www.civilbeat.org/2020/06/what-implicit-bias-looks-like-in-hawaii/

K. P., Manojan. "Capturing the Gramscian Project in Critical Pedagogy: Towards a Philosophy of Praxis in Education." *Review of Development and Change*, vol. 24, no. 1, June 2019, pp. 123–145, doi:10.1177/0972266119831133. Accessed 31 March 2022.

Allens, David. "Dependency, White Privilege, and Transnational Hegemonic Reconfiguration: Investigating Systems of Power and Identity Privilege in The Bahamas." *Caribbean Quilt*, vol 5, May 2020.

Aluli Meyer, Manulani. "Ho'oulu: Our Time of Becoming," Honolulu, HI: 'Ai Pōhaku Press, 2003.

Smith, Sharon. "Black Feminism and Intersectionality", issue 91, 1 September 2021. Accessed 2 April 22.

Beamer, Lorenz Gonschor Kamanamaikalani. "Toward an Inventory of Ahupua'a in the Hawaiian Kingdom: A survey of Nineteenth and early Twentieth-Century Cartographic and Archival Records of the Island of Hawai'i." *The Hawaiian Journal of History*, vol. 48, 2014, p 79.

Lee, Suevon. "How 12 Teens Who'd Never Met Before Organized Honolulu's Black Lives Matter Protest." *Civil Beat*, 22 June 2020. https://www.civilbeat.org/2020/06/how-12-teens-whod-never-met-before-organized-honolulus-Black-lives-matter-protest/. Accessed 22 March 2022.

Chammah, Maurice And Aspinwall, Cary. "The Short, Fraught History Of The 'Thin Blue Line' American Flag." *Politico* Magazine, 9 June 2020. https://www.politico.com/news/magazine/2020/06/09/the-short-fraught-history-of-the-thin-blue-line-american-flag-309767

Wang C, Burris MA. "Photovoice: Concept, Methodology, and Use for Participatory Needs Assessment." Health Education & Behavior. 1997, p. 369

Bunn, Curtis. "Report: Black people are still killed by police at a higher rate than other groups." https://www.nbcnews.com/news/nbcblk/report-black-people-are-still-killed-police-higher-rate-groups-rcna17169 Accessed 29 December 2022

www.ingramcontent.com/pod-product-compliance
Lightning Source LLC
Chambersburg PA
CBHW071744270326
41928CB00013B/2796